"Extreme weather events, oil spills, bank failures, massive tech shifts, cyber attacks and terrorist attacks, civil unrest, epidemics and pandemics, asset bubbles, fiscal crises, and energy price shocks. Organizations are operating in increasingly complex and turbulent worlds that require them to navigate chaos and the dynamics of change. Leveraging positive organizational energy, collective design thinking and strategic super-flexibility, Tkaczyk provides an alternative paradigm for organizational change and development. Energize-Redesign-Gel (ERG), human-centered and business-focused, is a powerful design-inspired strategy for re-imagining your business and leading positive organizational change. Filled with ready-to-use worksheets, tools and templates (You'll save hours of time!), it's ideal for executive and change leadership teams. A brilliant sourcebook!"

– MARSHALL GOLDSMITH, New York Times and
Wall Street Journal best-selling author

"Organizations with deep learning cultures are shown to be more competitive and successful in the marketplace. What's great about Bart's work is that he recognizes the role that learning and development can play in affecting positive change in people and companies. In *Leading Positive Organizational Change*, Bart introduces a new framework that involves a cycle of positive action and strategic learning that leads to sustained and effective change. And then he takes the framework and offers imminently practical and easy-to-use resources that can help any team create successful change efforts. This book will help many organizations emerge from the challenging times of today better than they were before."

– TONY BINGHAM, President and CEO, Association
for Talent Development (ATD)

"Like no other scholar, Bart Tkaczyk knows in his writings how to touch the head, the heart and the hands! With *Leading Positive Organizational Change*, he not only offers a conceptual model in three chapters that most OD practitioners will recognize and will help them in their daily practice to understand what change processes evoke in their organization. On top of that, the book provides the reader with a ToolBox of 30 tools to apply the model in their own jobs! Tkaczyk's book is a 'must read' and even more so a 'must use' book for anyone who is involved with leading change in their organization!"

– DIRK BUYENS, Professor of Human Resources and
Partner of Vlerick Business School, Head of the HR
Centre and Director of the Open Executive Education
Programs at Vlerick Business School

"The model and practices in this book represent, perhaps better than any other resource today, the effective blending of sound theory and relevant practice on the topic of change leadership. The literature on this topic abounds with approaches taken from a dizzying array of perspectives, often based on limited practice and devoid of any deeper understandings. In the end, the anchor of good practice often comes from seeking out enduring principles and finding ways to make them useful. From this perspective, Tkaczyk's work continues to demonstrate the important contributions of the informed scholar-practitioner in the management and human resources fields. Certainly, the book will impact the actions of global managers seeking to lead the change process in organizations in more predictable and reliable ways."

– RONALD L. JACOBS, Professor, Human Resource Development, University of Illinois, Urbana-Champaign, Principal, RL Jacobs & Associates, former President of Academy of Human Resource Development (AHRD)

"Dr. Bart Tkaczyk continues to deliver yet another typically pragmatic message dealing with effective organizational development, based on sound academic foundations involving strategic management approaches coupled with positive leadership. What distinguishes this new offering, compared to writings by others employing similar managerial catchwords, is his ability to inject a dramatic input of practicality into the mode of delivering procedures for change that are original, workable, understandable and effective by means of a 'Toolbox Modality'. On this you have my word!"

– PHILIP NECK, Southern Cross University, Australia, former Head of Entrepreneurship and Management Development, the United Nations International Labour Organization HQ, Geneva

"The book by Dr. Bart Tkaczyk advances our understanding of the process of instigating and sustaining a positive organizational change. It elucidates the underlying factors and dynamics that yet are rather underexplored and thus brings about unique added value for both scholars and practitioners."

– SHLOMO TARBA, Chair in Strategy and International Business, Birmingham Business School, the University of Birmingham, UK, Deputy Editor-in-Chief of British Journal of Management, Fellow of the Academy of Social Sciences

"Too many books in this market are more theoretical, but the ToolBox makes this one really good for someone wanting help in actually doing OD ... A short book with good tools that could be used as a practical additional text in either an OD or HRM class."

– PATRICK M. WRIGHT, Thomas C. Vandiver Bicentennial Chair in Business, Director of the Center for Executive Succession, Darla Moore School of Business, University of South Carolina

"This is a refreshing new angle on a topic that requires almost by definition energy and genuine enthusiasm. Dr. Bart Tkaczyk writes with feeling and an almost religious zeal but the material is all the more welcome for it. There are great insights here. Very definitely highly recommended!"

– MOORAD CHOUDHRY, former CEO of Habib Bank AG Zurich, Head of Treasury at Royal Bank of Scotland, Head of Treasury at Europe Arab Bank, Head of Treasury at KBC, Vice President at JP Morgan Chase Bank

"In his change consulting and coaching, Dr. Bart Tkaczyk combines a positive, practical, strengths-based approach with his extensive international experience and perspective, and his impressive and ongoing academic achievements. The results are excellent. At our company, we practice what Dr. Tkaczyk evangelizes."

– ALEXANDER HEHMEYER, Chairman of the Board, Advisor, and CFO at Rootstock Software

"Dr. Bart Tkaczyk lives and breathes positive Organization Development (OD). He's like a walking reference guide as well as an experienced practitioner and his eclectic mix of international work brings a uniquely different perspective. Throw out the old organizational change playbook – learn how to lead positive organizational change in a rigorous and creative way – the ERG way!"

– CRAIG FERGUSSON, Chartered MCIPD, former Associate Director, HR at Principles for Responsible Investment (PRI), an investor initiative in partnership with the United Nations Finance Initiative (UNEP FI) and the United Nations Global Compact

"ERG is well worth using."

– PRINCE MICHAEL VON LIECHTENSTEIN

"As Professor of Leadership Communications at the Haas School of Business, I cannot speak highly enough of the ERG model created by Dr. Bart Tkaczyk. As a fellow Fulbright Scholar, I know for a fact that Dr. Tkaczyk has combined elements of positive leadership, organizational culture, organization development and executive coaching to provide corporations, organizations, and individuals with a methodology that enables them to achieve positive organizational change. Any client will find Dr. Tkaczyk's approach unique and customized to fit their needs. Clients can look forward to a personalized relationship with him and his team enabling them to realize their bold goals and winning aspirations."

– MARK RITTENBERG, Haas School of Business, University of California, Berkeley

"Dr. Bart Tkaczyk is passionate about leadership and implementing change in a positive and impactful manner. If I could summarize him in three words it would be – energetic problem-solver."

– DEANNA ROCKEFELLER, Global Technology and Workforce Development Partnerships, Lockheed Martin

"The book follows Drucker's famous statement: plans are only good intentions unless they immediately degenerate into hard work. With a workbook included, it not only provides the theory but concrete guidance for action. In turbulent times we need to see innovation in the practice of management – to which this book contributes."

– RICHARD STRAUB, founder and President, Global Peter Drucker Forum

"Leading Positive Organizational Change provides an innovative framework with an immensely helpful set of practical tools for navigating organizational change through radically changing times. The ERG approach synthesizes and builds on the latest research in positive organizational scholarship (POS), addressing a crucial need in this time of turbulence and unrest. It's an energizing book and an invaluable asset for leaders and teams across a wide range of organizations."

– BRANDON VAIDYANATHAN, Associate Professor and Chair of the Department of Sociology at the Catholic University of America, Distinguished Fellow of the Ciocca Center for Principled Entrepreneurship in the Busch School of Business, Cornell University Press and Oxford University Press author

"As the cliché goes 'Change is the only constant'. If your organization is experiencing change by design or due to global turmoil, this book is a great guide to tide over the changes. It will help any organization go through a framework model to negotiate the change and bring about a positive outlook both in the organizations and its individuals. The book brings in a new way of thinking and applying this critical thinking in practice."

– CHERIAN VARGHESE, Regional Managing Director and VP of ASEAN & South Asian Growing Economies (SAGE) at Oracle

"A concise book packed with both theoretical and practical insights, *Leading Positive Organizational Change* couldn't have been a more timely resource for leaders and companies in such turbulent times as these. Tkaczyk offers a reflective yet empirically-relevant discourse about the way organizations could be (re)energized to shift from status quo to significance through an explorative, developmental, and interventional approach to change. If you are looking for a proven model of change that drives positive results in current, complex times, this book is the secret sauce. It will definitely change the way you view change. The impact is one of positive deviance – mindset, behavioral, and organizational change!"

– ROLAND K. YEO, Strategic HR
Advisor, Saudi Aramco,
Stanford University Press author

Leading Positive Organizational Change

Although many organizations see the need to transform and to reinvent themselves, for far too many leaders, "change" and "failure" are virtual synonyms. In fact, most organizational change efforts fail. But that needn't be the case, and help is at hand. *Leading Positive Organizational Change,* an alternative way to think about organizational change and development, is a strategic, learnable discipline that can re-energize and re-imagine your enterprise, and release the potential for change – delivering a positive, creative future and breakthrough bottom-line results.

Written by an award-winning expert in positive organization development and change leadership, this book provides executives, change leaders, and change leadership teams with a step-by-step guide to collaboratively crafting and executing a change strategy that aligns with organizational objectives so as to fuel their future. With a strong science-backed and field-tested "how to" approach, and with a radical focus on organizational positivity, super-flexibility and renewal, collective design thinking and applied imagination, this highly practical book features:

- A **ToolBox** of 30 powerful, imaginative (and *time-saving*!) tools for you to use in practicing leading *positive* organizational change and carrying through your change program – with example templates and worksheets, concise notes and ideas from numerous complex global projects.
- **Lead-ins** to each chapter that are a fundamental feature of the book, representing a springboard to a chapter and serving the purpose of awakening interest in the topic.
- **Dialogic Reflection for Professional Team Development**, at the start of each chapter, that enables you (and your team as a whole) to reflect on and discuss some thought-provoking questions, linking to the chapter and helping to contextualize your learning.
- **Industry Snapshots** that explore current issues and trends in one of the fastest-growing professions and industries – coaching and consulting.
- **Windows on Practice** that demonstrate how issues are applied in real-life business situations, offering a range of interesting topical illustrations of positive change leadership in practice, relating the core concepts of the book to real-world settings.

- **Summary Propositions**, at the end of each chapter, that recap and reinforce the key takeaways from the chapter.
- **References** to help you take your learning and development further.

Tkaczyk's engaging, reflective, task-based book equips the change leader and leadership teams with the skills needed to navigate chaos and the unexpected, to renew your business and create winning change. This action-based workbook can be used in a variety of business settings, among others, executive leadership team meetings, organization development and change consulting, design-led strategy retreats, human resource development consultancy, executive 1:1 and team coaching, leadership boot camps, design thinking workshops and sprints, innovation labs, and executive education and MBA courses – as a handy additional text in either an organization development and change or human resource management class. It can also be used in a flexible strategic transformation program – with the flow of the change execution process mapped within the context of a specific change initiative.

Bart Tkaczyk, a Fulbright Scholar at the University of California at Berkeley, and a Managing Member with Energizers, LLC, an award-winning American strategic transformation consulting firm, is a trusted strategy advisor to major corporations and governments worldwide, a professional executive coach and executive educator, and a sought-after speaker. Visit www.drtkaczyk.com Email bart_tkaczyk@berkeley.edu Follow on Twitter DrBTkaczykMBA.

Leading Positive Organizational Change

Energize – Redesign – Gel

Bart Tkaczyk

Routledge
Taylor & Francis Group

LONDON AND NEW YORK

First published 2021
by Routledge
2 Park Square, Milton Park, Abingdon, Oxon OX14 4RN

and by Routledge
52 Vanderbilt Avenue, New York, NY 10017

Routledge is an imprint of the Taylor & Francis Group, an informa business

British Library Cataloguing-in-Publication Data
A catalogue record for this book is available from the British Library

Library of Congress Cataloging-in-Publication Data
A catalog record has been requested for this book

ISBN: 978-0-367-90347-3 (hbk)
ISBN: 978-0-367-60876-7 (pbk)
ISBN: 978-1-003-02393-7 (ebk)

Typeset in Times New Roman
by codeMantra

Access the Support Material: www.routledge.com/9780367608767

Mom and Dad, genuine positive energizers, to whom I owe my greatest debt

Contents

Acknowledgments

This book would not have been possible without the support of my wonderful family (who keep me humble) and dear friends (who keep me sane). I'm feeling so energized and deeply thankful to have you, and that you *never* tired of asking me, "Have you finished that book yet?"

Rick Bagozzi, for being an inspiration, and for being an amazingly generous and caring academic mentor.

Jennifer Koerber Miller and Dominik Wieczorek, my life coaches, for constant energy boosts along the way.

Writing a book is a major production. I actually started to craft it in Bournemouth (UK) in 2013 and I finished writing it in Berkeley, California (US) in 2020. I was extremely fortunate to have a brilliant editorial team at Routledge, both in Milton Park, Abingdon, Oxfordshire (UK) and in New York, NY (US): Susan Dunsmore, Ed Gibbons, Rebecca Marsh, Sophie Peoples, and Megan A. Smith, who were wonderfully supportive (and endlessly patient – every time I stretched the delivery deadlines). I am also genuinely grateful to Mary C. Gentile (University of Virginia Darden School of Business) for initially reading over the book proposal, and for connecting me with Routledge in 2017.

Enormous appreciation goes to the distinguished book reviewers and endorsers: Tony Bingham, Dirk Buyens, Moorad Choudhry, Craig Fergusson, Marshall Goldsmith, Alex and Carol Hehmeyer, Ron Jacobs, Prince Michael of Liechtenstein, Phil Neck, Mark Rittenberg, Deanna Rockefeller, Richard Straub, Shlomo Tarba, Brandon Vaidyanathan, Cherian Varghese, Patrick M. Wright, and Roland K. Yeo, who read an early draft of the book and offered opinions about various sections, and given their level of talent and the generosity of the time they gave me, this really should be a lot better book. You are so kind, and you are my role models.

Jack Dunster, who has now read and edited every word of what I have written. If Jack ever publishes a book, just buy it. It will be fantastic.

Continuous learning and development is a journey with a potential to take one from where one is now to places one has only imagined and even places one never thought one would reach. Within the educational space, I owe much to the University of California, Berkeley-Haas School of Business (especially Homa Bahrami, Rich Lyons, Mark Rittenberg, and Paul Tiffany), Birkbeck, University of London (especially Alistair Cumming, Julie Davies, Philip Dewe, Roger Fagg, J.C. Gacilo, Bex Hewitt, Erica Levy, Andreas Liefooghe, Almuth McDowall, Katrina Pritchard, and Patrick Tissington), University College London (especially Karol Wyszynski), the University of Illinois at Urbana-Champaign (especially Alexandre Ardichvili, Jeff Flesher, Ron Jacobs, Scott Johnson, Russ Korte, Peter Kuchinke, James A. Leach, and Tod Treat), the University of Minnesota's Carlson School of Management (especially Toby Nord, and Virajita Singh), Ivey Business School-Western University (especially Darren Meister), and the University of Toronto's Rotman School of Management (especially Roger Martin, Avi Goldfarb, Jennifer Riel, Stefanie Schram, and Avni Shah).

The ideas in the book were also strengthened by ongoing discussions with great friends and colleagues of the Academy of Management (AOM), the Association for Talent Development (ATD), the Bahrain Society for Training & Development (BSTD), the British Academy of Management (BAM), the Chartered Institute of Personnel and Development (CIPD), the Design Management Institute (DMI), International Federation of Training and Development Organisations (IFTDO), the Krynica Economic Forum, the United States Department of State (DOS), and the United Nations (UN).

Specifically, I would like to acknowledge colleagues at the United Nations who keep leading positive change, especially António Guterres (United Nations Secretary-General), Jeffrey A. Brez (Chief, NGO Relations, Advocacy & Special Events, Department of Public Information), Elizabeth M. Cousens (the President and CEO of the United Nations Foundation), Elliott Harris (Assistant Secretary-General for Economic Development and Chief Economist), Bruce Knotts (Chair, NGO DPI Executive Committee), Maher Nasser (Director of the Outreach Division in the Department of Global Communications and Commissioner-General of the UN at Expo 2020), and Natalie Samarasinghe (Executive Director, the United Nations Association – UK).

Last but not least, I would like express my sincere gratitude to all the clients, executives, executive leadership teams (ELTs), and MBAs worldwide for helping me shape and, rigorously *and* experimentally, field-test the selected concepts, tools, and practices in the book.

Thank you very much to all – I truly appreciate you. Keep on energizing!

Abbreviations

ADT	Attention Deficit Trait
AHRD	Academy of Human Resource Development
AI	artificial intelligence
AOM	Academy of Management
ASTD	American Society for Training & Development
ATD	Association for Talent Development
BAM	British Academy of Management
BLS	U.S. Bureau of Labor Statistics
BPR	business process reengineering
Brexit	the withdrawal of the United Kingdom from the European Union
BSTD	Bahrain Society for Training & Development
CEE	Central and Eastern Europe
CEO	chief executive officer
CFO	chief financial officer
CHRO	chief human resource officer
CIPD	Chartered Institute of Personnel and Development
CITO	chief information technology officer
CMC-Canada	Canadian Association of Management Consultants
COVID-19	Coronavirus disease 2019
CPD	continuing professional development
CQ	cultural intelligence
DMI	Design Management Institute
DOS	U.S. Department of State
DT	design thinking
DX	digital transformation
EAP	employee assistance program
ELT	executive leadership team
ERG	energize, redesign, and gel
ERP	enterprise resource planning
EQ	emotional intelligence
EU	European Union

FEACO	Fédération Européenne des Associations de Conseils en Organisation (European Federation of Management Consultancies Associations)
FTSE	Russell FTSE Group and Frank Russell Company
GCC	Gulf Cooperation Council
GDP	gross domestic product
HCI	Human Capital Institute
HMD	Human Mortality Database
HR	human resources
HRD	human resource development
HRM	human resource management
ICE	individual coaching for effectiveness
ICF	International Coach Federation
IFTDO	International Federation of Training and Development Organisations
IOC	integrated oil company
IT	information technology
L&D	learning and development
M&A	mergers and acquisitions
MBA	Master of Business Administration
MBO	management by objectives
MCA	Management Consultancies Association
NTP	National Transformation Program
O&G	oil and gas
OD	organization development
PERT	program evaluation and review technique
PM	personnel management
PMI	Personal Management Interview
POB	positive organizational behavior
POS	positive organizational scholarship
PsyCap	psychological capital
ROE	return on expectations
ROI	return on investment
SDGs	sustainable development goals
SME	small and medium-sized enterprise
SOAR	strengths, opportunities, aspirations, and results
TD	talent development
TQM	total quality management
UAE	United Arab Emirates
UK	United Kingdom
UN	United Nations
US	United States
VUCA	volatility, uncertainty, complexity, and ambiguity

Introduction

In today's challenging and turbulent times, leading change, whether in your organization or personal life, is not easy. Study after study after study have revealed that the failure rate of organizational change programs is alarmingly high – around 70 percent – irrespective of whether they are driven by mergers, acquisitions, de-layering, IT, total quality management, business process re-engineering, downsizing, or culture change efforts. It is thus little wonder that people feel de-energized, uninspired and unmotivated by traditional change management ...

Nevertheless, why do some enterprises (think: Apple Inc., Capital One Financial Corporation, the Coca-Cola Company, Four Seasons Hotels and Resorts, Intuit Inc., the Lego Group, or the Walt Disney Company) succeed in leading and executing transformational change and in managing "surprises" while others mismanage the unexpected and fail miserably? *What if* we stopped practicing (and spinning our wheels) the same old deficits-based organizational change management tactics that revolve forever around *what fails*, and focused on *what works* instead?

Combining theory and real-world examples, fusing a science-backed methodology with applied imagination, this book, consisting of two parts, has this very specific purpose and gives a practical exhibition and explanation of how the application of leading *positive* organizational change can help you and your team navigate chaos and disruption, scaling and growth, change successfully, and fuel your future.

The structure of the book

Part I, "Understanding the practice of leading *positive* organizational change," is composed of three chapters, is about leading *positive* organizational change as a *practice* – what it is and why (Chapter 1), how it is applied to team coaching (Chapter 2), and how it is applicable to strategic human resource and organization development consulting (Chapter 3).

Chapter 1, "An alternative strategy for leading *positive* organizational change: Energize, Redesign, and Gel (ERG)," introduces the Energize, Redesign, and Gel (ERG) framework. ERG, a research-based and practice-informed discipline, is a cycle of positive action and strategic learning over time that leads to sustained and effective change. Specifically, the focus here is on: the "positive" (energizing the workplace, enhancing organizational health and renewal), "design" (putting into place collective design thinking and appreciative future search), and "organizational ambidexterity" (thriving on fluid reality and super-flexibly adapting to change), so as to deliver the desired future and breakthrough bottom-line results.

Chapter 2, "Team coaching for *positive* organizational change: building and sustaining high-quality teams via ERG," demonstrates how *team-centered* coaching, grounded in *dialogic* organization development and behavioral science, is an ideal mechanism for accelerating and sustaining positive change and engagement. Moreover, making use of generative coaching conversations around change issues can help enterprises to strategize more openly, and to create new awareness, behaviors, possibilities, and outcomes. As showcased in this chapter, getting from dilemma to solution is strategic, and it requires imaginative responses within a team-focused coaching methodology built on a team charter; a cycle of energizing, redesigning, and gelling; and a dialogic approach to learning.

Chapter 3, "ERG strategizing: a professional approach to *positive* human resource and organization development consulting," to capture its full potential, illustrates how a comprehensive and systematic *diagnostic* organization development can be strategically integrated with genuinely effective dialogic organization development to create a potent change process. To further offer practical insight into how issues are tackled in real-life organizational situations, this chapter reports on how positive organization change was facilitated in a methodological and experimental way by means of the ERG method, within the training department of a company – with the aid of a strategic human resource development consultancy. Specifically, the positive transformation account records one organizational development and change effort, i.e., going from a rigid training function, to *knowledge-creative* learning and development – and strategically aligning the new learning and development with business so as to effectively execute the organization's strategy and renew their enterprise. The *diagnostic-dialogic* extension of the organization development approach to change is particularly successful in a volatile, uncertain, complex, and ambitious (VUCA) world of continual change. It positions strategic organization development optimally to be able to positively impact how change in organizations is led, to harness uncertainty and to get ready for tomorrow. This chapter also serves as an introduction to the world of consulting – an industry and profession that are alluring (and misunderstood), yet highly competitive.

Part II, "Tools and templates for the practice of leading *positive* organizational change," introduces the ToolBox, anchored in the applied imagination methodology, which is a collection of 30 powerful, design thinking-based (and time-saving!) tools for practicing leading *positive* organizational change, with some example templates, concise notes and ideas from very many projects worldwide. The tools will help to evoke imagination and ask better questions that defy dusty answers (and perhaps question some existing organizational assumptions), so as to develop new creative knowledge and fully realize your organization's ideas and impact, remaking your enterprise into a game-changer.

Rather than industry-specific processes, this part of the book focuses on developing project-specific change interventions that can be field-tested and developed through real-world applications. This *positively deviant* methodology, rather than narrowing its horizons to the practice of mono-disciplinary inquiry, foregrounds both reflective individual projects and teamwork, stakeholder engagement, human-centered ethos, people-first empathetic innovation, visualization, improvising, storytelling, continuous learning, and peer learning, practicing guided imagery, progressive design thinking and doing, thinking in metaphors and analogies, journey mapping, (re)framing, ideating, rapid prototyping and iterative testing, among others, by embracing multi-disciplinary and active collaboration.

This task-based part of the book, called the ToolBox, through 30 activities, promoting using field research as a creative tool, will re-energize and open what is bubbling near the surface of the imagination in order to develop the skills needed for leading and thriving amidst change, make your team super-flexible and build up the leadership team's capacity for navigating the dynamics of change that is driven by both dialogue and diagnosis. To jump-start *positive* change, the handy and resourceful ToolBox, *à la* Workbox, contains 30 tools for you to use in carrying through your change project:

- the ENERGIZE WorkBox (10 tools)
- the REDESIGN WorkBox (10 tools)
- the GEL WorkBox (10 tools)

This selection of customizable and fillable tools in the designerly ToolBox is by no means exhaustive, but these are the ready-to-use resources that other global change leaders, working for Fortune 500 companies, SMEs, government and social-sector organizations, have found extremely stimulating and immediately practical when leading their organizations through an unanticipated but positive shift, applying the learnable, award-winning ERG method. Indeed, they have been designed to take you outside of the usual conventions of creativity, specialized disciplinary training, or cultural conditioning.

Importantly, even if I have written this book mainly for practitioners (for *teams* in particular), my research, for many years, has also sought to advance new theory on leading organizational change with numerous en-terprises across a wide spectrum of sectors and geographies. In terms of a research strategy, to explore the phenomenon within a number of real-life contexts and to actually develop a deeper understanding of the contexts of the research and the processes being enacted, I have typically adopted a multiple *case study* strategy. To collect and analyze data, I have employed both qualitative and quantitative research methods such as interviews, observation, documentary review and analysis, surveys, and questionnaires, among others. Multiple sources of data were used and triangulated (*triangulation* in this sense means applying different data collection techniques within one case study in order to make certain that the data tells one what one thinks it is telling, for instance, qualitative data collected by means of semi-structured interviews is a useful way of triangulating quantitative data collected through, say, a questionnaire). Although intensive and demanding by nature, the case study strategy has helped to generate answers to "why" questions, as well as "what" and "how" questions, and incorporating multiple cases has enabled the findings to be replicated across cases. I hope that this work on leading *positive* organizational change will be a useful source of further research avenues for interested strategic transformation scholars.

A final note

A final note on actively using this book: *We work in teams, right? So... why don't we read books and learn in teams?* To get the best learning out of this change leadership book, I encourage you to experiment and to actually "do" this book actively with a colleague or with your team-members. You should actually include the whole organization in visioning for the future. The idea is to include everybody in the process of change not just the notification of change. Therefore, I recommend that your team as a whole get engaged and join in the fun, read and work through the book together. Why not use your peers as sources of knowledge? For example, in your team, reflect on thought questions in the Dialogic Reflection for Professional Team Development sections; discuss Windows on Practice, Industry Snapshots, and Summary Propositions; explore the References; write in fillable templates in the ToolBox; doodle and draw your way through this *learn-by-doing* book packed with creative things to do. In other words, you and your team should puzzle things out and learn BIG–together.

Ultimately, this way you will evolve as a curious learner, as a reflexive practitioner, as a flexible collaborator and as a design-led and inspired strategist. By applying the notions and ideas found within this book, you will be equipped to both embrace fully what can often feel like chaos (turning every transformation program into success), and to co-create new paradigms–and a positive, progressive future!

Enjoy your *positive* change journey!

Warmly,

Bart Tkaczyk
London and San Francisco
drtkaczyk.com
bart_tkaczyk@berkeley.edu
twitter.com/DrBTkaczykMBA

Part I

Understanding the practice of leading *positive* organizational change

1 An alternative strategy for leading *positive* organizational change

Energize, redesign, and gel (ERG)

Lead-in

There is nothing permanent except change, and many change initiatives fail. The pushes propelling organizations and their leaders toward change come from the outside (think environmental pressures such as geopolitics, climate changes, epidemics and pandemics, work automation, industry disruption, or hypercompetition) and/or the inside (think organizational pushes like change of leadership, adopting new technology, organizational identity or growth pressures). Executing strategic transformations successfully in a world in which *volatility, uncertainty, complexity,* and *ambiguity* (VUCA) reign is difficult – the failure rate of change efforts is around 70 percent. Therefore, to lead *positive* organizational change, be catalysts for adaptability, and be continuously change-ready, executive leadership teams, today, need new dynamic capabilities, methods and skills that go beyond managing, namely, energizing, redesigning, and gelling (ERG). ERG is a cycle of action and learning over time that leads to sustained and effective change and organizational renewal. Specifically, the focus here is on: the "positive" (energizing the workplace, enhancing organizational health), "design" (putting into place collective design thinking and appreciative future search), and "organizational ambidexterity" (thriving on fluid reality and adapting to change super-flexibly), so as to bring forth a golden future for, and health and prosperity within, the enterprise.

Dialogic reflection for professional team development

In your team, discuss the following questions:

1. Why do so many change initiatives fail so often?
2. If a major change program had to be implemented in your enterprise, what do you think would be the major barriers that would stand in its

way, and what can you and your organization do to remove (some of) those barriers?

3. Do you know some popular theoretical frameworks that can help guide the change process and management effectively?

4. What are continuously change-ready and learning-ready enterprises very good at doing?

5. "Change should be planned and dictated from the top. When the change is announced, frontline employees *will* just go along and deliver it." Do you agree or disagree with this statement?

6. Now, reflect upon your own approach to leading change so as to deliver a creative future. How would you describe your role as a change leader (e.g., as a change architect, catalyst, challenger, team coach, connector, designer, director, dreamer, positive energizer, explorer, futurist, disruptive innovator, insider expert, interpreter, mentor, monitor, navigator, negotiator, networker, nurturer, socializer, storyteller, cultural steward, teacher, digital transformer, or a trusted advisor)?

> *If you want something new, you have to stop doing something old.*
> (Peter F. Drucker, a giant in the development
> of management thinking)

The one permanent feature in our times is *change*. Andy Grove, the former President and Chief Executive Officer (CEO) of Intel, holds forth that change is never-ending and is constantly and endlessly accelerating (Grove, 1999). The pace of change is furious and businesses are bashed about as rocks are battered by the sea. Still, it must be recognized that such change differs in terms of type and scale. Herein, change could be large-scale and radical and transformative – even to the roots of the organization and to the ways it operates. Such change can involve merger and acquisition (M&A) transactions, the workplace technology, or organizational restructuring and downsizing. Change could also be small-scale and incremental. Change of this nature involves being flexible in activity and the market, practicing continuous process improvement, fine-tuning business endeavors and employee and client relationships. These practices support organizational continuity. Still, change leadership, like riding a bucking bronco, is not successful without effort, whether these changes are continuous or episodic, planned or unplanned, radical or small-scale, continuous and incremental or discontinuous, reactive or anticipatory, revolutionary or adaptive, or tectonic and volcanic, as exemplified right now.

Change is fierce: important lessons from the field

It can truthfully be said that the majority of businesses that are now more than ten years old are different to what they were even as little as five years ago. Indeed, next year, they might be different to what they are this year. Organizations change for many reasons (e.g. the global financial crisis, team leadership transition, epidemics and pandemics, disruptive innovation, new ways of doing business and new ways of working, global expansion, recession, strategic changes, environmental and climate concerns, adopting new technology, work automation, paradigm shifts, changing consumer expectations, emerging new markets, and so on), but what is important is to always be ready for changes that might be desired or forced. The shove, the push for change can come from the outside (environmental) and/or from the inside (organizational).

The outside forces can be vigorous. First, the "power of individuals" is growing, with millennials and Generation Z at the forefront, who value collaboration, resourcefulness and transparency and who expect enterprises to make a positive social and environmental impact on society. For example, 51 percent of millennials would pay extra for sustainable products, and 49 percent of them prefer to work for a sustainable company (Nielsen, 2014). This goes far beyond "corporate responsibility" into really becoming a *conscious* capitalist and a *better* corporate citizen, and redefining value propositions in this way (Nooyi & Govindarajan, 2020). Therefore, nowadays, a good deal of organizations are making a purposeful effort to put sustainable practices into action, such as working toward the Sustainable Development Goals (SDGs) adopted by the United Nations in 2015 (UN, 2015). The good organization, whose purpose marries revenue growth and profit-making well with the need to be mindful of its environment and stakeholder ecosystem, knows that doing well by doing good not only helps the natural world and the general public, but it can also positively contribute to their brands' health and performance. Yes, "green" plans can help to save costs and the planet – minimizing packaging, cutting transportation costs, and placing energy-efficient lighting are some of the ways environmentally-savvy enterprises can lower costs. Yet, the bottom line is not only about profitability – it's about a culture change too.

On the subject of age and "social reconfiguration," the majority of kids born in affluent countries today can expect to live to be more than a 100, according to the Human Mortality Database (HMD, 2007). Rising life expectancies and an aging global workforce have been noticed for some time now but we still organize our lives the way our parents or grandparents did. In truth, current HR practices and policies are ill-equipped to navigate a 100-year life. Thus, the "longevity dividend" actually enables enterprises to partner with older workers to better craft new talent management strategies, to re-conceptualize work-life integration, to delink pay with age, to delay retirement, to tap into diverse networks and regenerative relationships, to design new learning and development opportunities, and to champion new multistage career models and experiences, as we will have to work a lot longer than our parents (Gratton & Scott, 2016).

Next, citizens seem to "trust business" more than government, globally. Clearly, 76 percent of the general population believe it is critically important for CEOs to respond to turbulent times and take the lead on change instead of waiting for government to impose it (Edelman, 2019). As a result, people are looking to business to fill the void on "wicked problems" like health-care. By way of illustration, Amazon, Berkshire Hathaway, and JP Morgan Chase joined forces to tackle employees' healthcare costs, addressing an issue that government cannot find a solution to on its own (Johnson, 2018).

Besides, rapid technological change, "automation" in particular, is exerting a profound impact on corporations and markedly altering the ways we work. That being the case, many jobs may be at risk of being automated within, say, the next 20 years, including numerous advisory jobs, such as medical consultants, lawyers, financial advisors, and management consultants. Yet, by leveraging human-automation collaboration and technology for sustainable growth, future-proof enterprises should be capitalizing on the benefits of Big Data, workplace connectivity, machine learning, and artificial intelligence (AI) (Agrawal *et al.*, 2018). The energy for embracing AI is widespread indeed. In point of fact, new research by MIT SMR Connections and SAS, based on 2,280 respondents, finds that AI implementation is transforming organizational culture and processes and creating new mandates for CEOs, chief information officers (CITOs), and other tech leaders. Specifically, 63 percent of the respondents expect AI/machine learning to drive dramatic or significant change, somewhat ahead of the cloud and well ahead of Internet-of-Things or blockchain. Besides, AI will require even more collaboration among employees trained in data management, analytics, IT infrastructure, and systems development, as well as business and operational experts. That being the case, organizational leaders will need to make sure that traditional silos will not stifle AI programs (MIT, 2020).

Among what can be considered as outside forces are "fad" pressures too. Under this banner are such notions as "fad-surfing" – chasing shiny baubles and embracing the latest "in-thing." This includes following ideas put forward by business gurus, such as management by objectives (MBO), international standardization, total quality management (TQM), program evaluation and review technique (PERT), proffering employee assistance programs (EAPs), business process reengineering (BPR), and enterprise resource planning (ERP). They also are notable in one company mimicking the change initiatives of others. This is evidenced in the action, in 2001, within Boeing Co. This enterprise, under the direction of CEO Philip Condit, slavishly followed the ways of Jack Welch, CEO at GE. Such undertakings embodied diversification into three core areas: finance, communication, and aircraft manufacture. Moreover, they relocated their headquarters from their manufacturing base in Seattle, Washington, to Chicago, Illinois, and established training and development in even another place – at St. Louis, Missouri (Greising, 2001). Whether this was good or bad in view of the 737 Max crisis, begs the question.

"Legal" pressures are another outside force affecting a company. Herein, legal pressures include lawsuits and court-ordered changes, for example, an organization being compelled to follow fair working or hiring practices. An instance of this is the pressure put upon Texaco through being the losing party in a lawsuit. The company ended up reorganizing its HR and diversity task forces, but first had to settle, in 1996, a significant class-action suit brought against it by current and former employees of African-American descent (over $170 million dollars) (Mulligan & Kraul, 1996).

"Geopolitical" pressures are one more outside force. By means of geopolitics, a one country-based model is often discovered to be not good enough for a company with global aspirations. 3M's experience exemplifies this. In the 1990s, to better interact with its Pan-European clients, it had to change its business model significantly from country-specific design, to regional and pan-European Union, with profit and loss control applied against all EU-based product lines as a whole (Ackenhusen *et al.*, 1996).

Outside forces also take in "market downtrend" pressures wherein a business is forced to downsize. Verizon Communications, for example, in 2002, had to let go some 3,500 technical/engineering staff due to the changes within the telecom sector (Zhao, 2002).

Moreover, "hypercompetition" pressures are found under the banner of outside forces as well. Due to this, businesses must always be prepared to examine and re-evaluate themselves in order to be in the forefront in their field. Dell, for example, in 2006, after 20 years of outstanding performance, met with an incredibly bad quarterly result – profits down 51 percent, while competitors HP and Lenovo enhanced their market share. The effect was due to Dell resting on its laurels, while its competitors hustled new and better products onto the market (Kirkpatrick, 2006).

"Reputational" pressures are yet one more outside pressure. In this regard, an organization is compelled to renew a damaged image after a scandal or because unethical activities or hidden quality control problems have come to light. In September of 2015, the Environmental Protection Agency realized that numerous Volkswagen cars offered for sale in the US had computer software in diesel engines that could detect when they were being tested, adjusting the performance suitably to boost results. The German automaker had since admitted cheating on emissions tests in the US. As a result of the emissions scandal, one of the most audacious corporate frauds in history, aka "Dieselgate," VW had to recall millions of cars worldwide from early in 2016, and it had to put aside €6.7 billion to finance costs. That led to its stock price falling in value by a third in the days immediately after the news, and the firm posting its first quarterly loss for 15 years of €2.5 billion in late October 2015 (Hotten, 2015).

Finally, we live in a world that's more interconnected than ever before, so a widespread occurrence of an infectious disease in one country or numerous countries at a particular time can become an "economic pandemic," changing our world – forever. Epidemics and pandemics generate widespread uncertainty and panic. As of this writing, the spread of the coronavirus disease (COVID-19) to so many places now makes this a global issue that can hurt economies, affect business continuity, slow spending, and upset the supply chain across different industries for months or years to come. Apple became the first major US company to report it will not meet its revenue projections for the current quarter due to the coronavirus outbreak. Volkswagen informed it would postpone production restarts at some Chinese plants. Fiat Chrysler Automobiles announced it, for the moment, had halted production in Serbia as it could not get parts from China, which continues to cope with manufacturing delays as it tries to contain the spread of the virus. A dearth of Chinese tourists in the US has also hit a number of luxury brands like Estée Lauder Cos. and Capri Holdings Ltd., which owns the Versace and Jimmy Choo brands (Mickle, 2020). Ultimately, for years, coronavirus will change how we shop, study, and travel, as well as how we do business. For example, companies will have to develop trust-based cultures with their staff. Remote working will become a lot more strategic and so in-person meetings will be less important. Businesses will have to be able to learn how to move faster, acting in more experimental and agile ways. Supply chain strategy will be rewritten. Physical components of offices, buildings, and public spaces will be redesigned so that indoor spaces drive performance and productivity too (Gerdeman, 2020).

The internal pushes can be intense as well. Inclusive among these are "new broom" pressures – personnel changes at the levels of the board and the CEO. Sears' Arthur Martinez, for instance, transformed Sears into a top-tier consumer brand and in doing so, closed down over 100 stores, got rid of their 100-year-old catalogue service and chose to market products oriented toward women (Sellers, 1997).

In addition, internal drives can take in pressures of change inside business entities that emerge from "below." Such change can *spiral upward* throughout the company and revolutionize and stimulate the way they work. This can often come about by means of the "issue-selling" process, e.g., companies discarding non-purpose-driven management practices. One notable case of this was that of a Silicon Valley-based innovator of high-performance networking technology, Juniper Networks. This enterprise, in 2011, dropped forced annual performance reviews and applied the notion of frequent "conversation days." The intent of such practices is to discuss personal development, goals, and holdbacks in a non-confrontational manner. This innovation had spiraled upwards from a young engineer employee in Bangalore, India, who felt that the company performance evaluation practices were demoralizing and held nothing positive for the business (Boudreau & Rice, 2015).

"Identity" pressures are another aspect of internal drives for change. Companies that are low on identity often re-invent themselves to build up business. The United States Mint typifies this. A shadowy federal organization responsible for making coin and paper currency, under Philip Diehl, it developed an excellent customer-focused identity. Indeed, on the American Customer Satisfaction Index, it scored second place – beaten only by Mercedes-Benz. Philip Diehl re-energized and changed everything – administrative operations, labor and management relations, and financial management. In doing so, he enhanced morale and the profitability of the entire establishment (Yoder, 1998).

"Growth pressure" is one more internal drive. This is exemplified by Apple Computing – once a start-up founded by Steve Jobs, it is now a huge player and a professionally managed enterprise, the change coming about under John Sculley, formerly of Pepsi-Cola and lured away to become Apple's CEO (Denning, 2011).

However, riding the bucking bronco of change is challenging. Transformations can fail. One major factor is "change fatigue." This is the act of being in a state of endless, multiple change that is without prioritization or chance to discover what works and what does not. Indeed, published statistics state that 61 percent of all enterprises undergo three or more changes a year, while some 26 percent have the ill pleasure to endure six or more change efforts. Beyond this horror, 45 percent opine that more change will be coming; yet 48 percent firmly believe the pace of change is too rapid and the results are unpredictable. Most enterprises also state they lack the expert skills to sustain long-term, continuous change. Of note, only 17 percent of all respondents rate their business entities as highly competent in managing change initiatives. Add to this that only 30 percent of all polled enterprises have professional change management teams (ASTD, 2014).

In the real world, approximately 70 percent of change initiatives are derailed or fall apart (Olson, 2008). As a further matter, transformations seem to be getting even riskier over time, as the success rate fell from roughly 30 percent in 2001 to 25 percent by 2012 (Reeves *et al.*, 2018). Such information is hidden and must be sussed out. Researchers have noted that, with regard to transformation, for every success, there is at least one proportionately sensational failure (Ghoshal & Bartlett, 1996).

Now, let us examine the statistics of four change cases: "downsizing," "mergers," "technological change," and managing the rise of the "virtual workplace". These are big change management challenges in today's environments that are volatile, uncertain, complex, and ambiguous (VUCA). Importantly, VUCA can be both an outcome of disruptive management innovation and a driver of it (Millar *et al.*, 2018).

1. *Downsizing*: When launching a restructuring by way of downsizing, cost-cutting through downsizing in the longer term may be a poor decision and a financially costly change effort. Actual academic study has indicated that while share prices go up on the announcement of downsizing, after two years, the shares lose their value (Cascio, 1993). Therefore, organizations, before deciding on downsizing, may want to first consider other alternatives and to ask themselves how they can actually change the way they do business, so that they can deploy the employees they now have more effectively. Essentially, be a responsible restructurer, i.e., view employees as assets to be developed rather than as costs to be cut (Cascio, 2002, Cascio *et al.*, 2020).

2. *Mergers*: The increasing popularity of mergers and acquisitions (M&A) as a collaborative method of strategic development and change (e.g., for growing in critical size and global reach) is manifested by the increasing scholarly attention refocused on the subject (Gomes, 2020; Gomes *et al.*, 2020). With regard to mergers, statistically, a favorable outcome is only achieved by 30 percent (Jordan & Stuart, 2000). In surveys conducted in recent years, the percentage of enterprises that failed to achieve the goals of the merger reached 83 percent (Weber *et al.*, 2014)! Perhaps applying new insights from *behavioral* economics could help out. For example, research suggests that the acquirer's risk-taking behavior and perception of merger synergies determine the price offered for the M&A transaction while the target firm's perception of synergies is less relevant (if at all) and their optimistic behavior is most useful, when the acquirer perceives high synergies existing in the potential M&A transaction (Agarwal & Kwan, 2018). Furthermore, loss aversion has a significant effect on this pricing with risk aversion and optimism also having some minor impact. However, the existence of multiple acquirers does positively increase the M&A transaction price (Agarwal *et al.*, 2018).

3. *Technological change*: As to technological change, in many major enterprises, IT can be a costly upheaval. Clients call helplines that are unhelpful. Orders get misplaced. Tracking systems do not track … As it happens, 20 percent of all capital earmarked for IT products and services do not seem to deliver their value. This adds up to around $500 billion wasted throughout the world (Feld & Stoddard, 2004). Nowadays, it looks like everyone is talking about setting out on a "digital business transformation" journey (Cennamo *et al.*, 2020). Yet, with no crystal-clear strategic direction, most companies (77 percent), in the digital economy, are *not* ready for a digital future (Weill & Woerner, 2018). Certainly, the digital era *is* a golden opportunity for organizations to renew and reinvent themselves, and for embracing digital disruption. As Thayde Olarte, VP, Consumer & Micro-Finance, International Banking, Scotiabank, shares:

> For any organization to embrace digital transformation, it has to start at the very top, so that the message cascades down. Having a CEO who is committed to digital transformation is very inspirational for people; but at the same time, as we say every day, everyone in the bank owns our digital transformation.
>
> (Crisp *et al.*, 2018: 55)

However, it must be remembered that when it comes to digital transformation, *digital* is not the key. *Transformation* is. Therefore, zero in on transformation, not on technology. Despite everything, it is possible that you do not lack a digital strategy. Perhaps you lack a better organizational renewal strategy, enabled by digital.

4. *Virtual organization design*: Finally, in the implementation of what is deemed "virtual organization design," global research (built upon the responses of 505 leaders occupying managerial positions or higher) indicates that while 99 percent of all respondents hold the belief that some or all of their white-collar staff can work virtually on an as-needed, set-schedule or full-time basis, only 21 percent admit that the organization they lead offers learning and development (L&D) programs for employees to adapt to such an environment (ASTD, 2013).

Due to extremely low success rates, scholars in this field have, thus, proposed a variety of change and transition management designs.

Change designs: three-step change models, according to Kurt Lewin and Karl Weick

Out of the vast field of change management frameworks (HBR, 2011), the two most dominant in the theory and practice of change management are that of Lewin (1947) and Weick (2000). Lewin's key contribution is in his change sequence:

1. "Unfreeze" (dismantling the present mindset).
2. "Move" (changing from less useful, to more useful sets of behaviors).
3. "Freeze" (ensuring that the new status quo is "refrozen" into or maintained within organizational operations and is made safe from reversion).

With regard to organization-wide planned change, Lewin's Three-Step Model is a conventionally applied approach to *organization development* (henceforth, "OD"). It is basically a catchall recipe for traditional, problem-solving-focused OD.

Karl Weick (2000) puts forward a constructive alternative to Lewin (the *sensemaking* theory of organizational change). In his proposition, the preferred change sequence is:

1. "Freeze" (capturing sequences, through cognitive maps and schemas).
2. "Rebalance" (reinterpreting, relabeling, or resequencing the patterns so that they unfold without difficulty).
3. "Unfreeze" (enabling further positive changes to occur).

In Weick-speak, sensemaking means "the making of sense" (Weick, 1995: 4). The notion encompasses "the ongoing retrospective development of plausible images that rationalize what people are doing" (Weick *et al.*, 2005: 409). Herein, management truly understands what the front line says and envisions the outcome of organizational change events. It can be said, thus, in Weick's model, management does not create change, it "certifies" it (Weick, 2000).

"Un/freeze" bugs in both designs

Design "bugs" exist in both of the aforementioned models (see Table 1.1 for quick reference).

Table 1.1 Design bugs in two classic three-stage models

Stage	Lewin (1947)	Design bugs	Weick (2000)	Design bugs
1	Unfreeze	In today's fast-paced environments, the system cannot be "unfrozen," as the system is not in a "frozen" state	Freeze	In practice, time cannot be completely "frozen" so as to eventually take part in "sensemaking," due to existing complex and accelerating internal and external dynamics
2	Move	"Moving" to new behaviors may be ineffective, especially when leading a large-scale, system-wide restructuring, if the "unfrozen" system is still not exactly "healthy"	Rebalance	The cognitive map or schema activated from the "frozen" image to be "rebalanced" may be outdated now. Plus, within the same organization, there will exist competing and conflicting cognitive representations, meanings, images, and interpretations of the same actions (business leaders' conceptual change frames and change announcements vs. individual employees' mental structures that orchestrate thought).
3	Freeze	"Freezing" is not "agile" enough for today	Unfreeze	By further "unfreezing," what is already working well could actually be disrupted

These are:

Bug 1: Regarding Lewin's model, Step 1 ("Unfreeze") is problematic. In the fast-paced business world of today, change is never-ending and its acceleration is driven by disruption. Enterprises live in a world wherein they and their competitors are fluctuating, emerging, clashing, shrinking, plummeting, dying, evolving, and booming. The system is, therefore, *already* "unfrozen."

Bug 2: In considering Weick's model, Step 3 ("Unfreeze") cannot be accepted without qualms. Attempts to keep the system unfrozen could disrupt a complex, adaptive system that actually functions well. Indeed, it begets the question as to whether change is necessary all the time, or does it engender chaos?

Bug 3: With respect to Step 3 in Lewin's model ("Freeze"), troublesome here is the assumption that business entities operate in a static state. They do not. The pot is boiling. Hence, "freezing" is not *agile* enough for the fast-changing business environment of today. Accordingly, a frozen state may be the worst scenario down the road.

Bug 4: Concerning Weick's Step 1 ("Freeze"), in business world reality, time cannot be completely frozen, because business ebbs and flows much as the ocean does. Since new knowledge or new organizational power, politics, and dynamics come about continuously, "sensemaking" cannot be paused – as the result of such activity is obsolete even as it is being undertaken.

Hence, both models are inadequate for today's hyperdynamic business world.

ERG: an alternative way to frame organization development and change

What is proposed here is a *positive* fix to both models: Lewin's (Table 1.2, part a) and Weick's (Table 1.2, part b). This too unfolds as three parts, however, it puts forward a new, *iterative* ERG change code (Table 1.2, part c). In accomplishing this, a clear and effective framework can be put in place to reconceptualize organizational change. In addition, an enterprise-wide common language for thinking about change can be embedded, and a playbook for disciplined transformation executions is cast. For explanatory purposes, this is set out as a staged process; in reality, it is a *dynamic* and *continuous* process. Furthermore, it is an aspect of the day-to-day routine that should be fundamental in the enterprise's business culture and in its strategy setting; this usually requires a shift in workplace culture and workplace learning culture, and new patterns of social organization.

Table 1.2 The evolution of three-stage models

Model	Stage 1	Stage 2	Stage 3	Theoretical perspective
(a) K. Lewin	Unfreeze	Move	Freeze	*Traditional* Organization Development
(b) K. Weick	Freeze	Rebalance	Unfreeze	Sensemaking
(c) B. Tkaczyk	Energize	Redesign	Gel	*Positive* Organizational Scholarship and Development/ *Design* Thinking/ *Super*-Flexibility

Part 1

Before reorganization, rather than "unfreezing" a system perceived as flawed (Lewin's Step 1), or cognitively "freezing" the situation in order to map it to make sense of it (Weick's Step 1), the organization and its change leaders need "energizing." Generating a positive culture is critical. Indeed, with regard to "positive energizers," high-performing enterprises have three times more such individuals than do the average (Baker, 2004; cited in Cameron, 2008: 43).

Those so-called "positive energizers" are people who energize the workplace and stimulate progress or put forward team initiatives. Such individuals are described as being more engaged, committed, proactive, energized, trustworthy, and unselfish (Baker *et al.*, 2003). They are not "energy-neutral" – committed to merely going with the flow, or "de-energizers" or "negative energizers," who stifle workplace initiatives and belittle their fellow workers. Negative energizers are seen to be more critical, inflexible, selfish, and unreliable (Cross *et al.*, 2003).

Organizational network analysis has discovered that a "positive energizer" is four times more likely to be successful than someone at the center of the "influence" or "information" network (Baker *et al.*, 2003). According to researchers, great leaders initially set in motion organizational energy, then channel it (Tushman & O'Reilly, 1996). Hence, organizational energy is both manageable and measurable (Bruch & Vogel, 2011).

Change leadership such as this can be developed methodologically and systematically, for example, through "self-managed learning" and *continuous* "learning by self-insight" (Tkaczyk, 2014a; 2014b). Change leaders, or, rather, "change energizers," are cognizant of organizational energy, particularly in the times of turbulence when organizations must strategize to utilize every asset in order to survive. Since organizational energy brings forth "the necessary combination of cognitive, emotional and action-taking capabilities and aligns the resulting force to achieve business goals" (Bruch & Ghoshal, 2003: 51), boosting and sustaining energy in the workplace are crucial.

Energy is *the* fuel that great enterprises run upon (Dutton, 2003a). Without positive energy, change cannot be successful. "Energizing" involves *purposeful* action ("crazy busyness" is one of the central hazards to meaningful action-taking). It also implies the construction of a compelling case for change, as well as firing up the enterprise, for example, by means of storytelling. Furthermore, it implies mobilizing key people – those who are comfortable with change, and who will hold onto their energy levels and momentum throughout the process of transformation. In addition, it includes engendering emotional buy-in to the idea of joining forces with company-wide departmental staff. Finally, it involves socializing positively and empathizing with others. All in all, it means establishing a humane, healthy, and vibrant workplace environment.

It must be recognized that an enterprise's human resources are human beings (rather than cogs in a machine) and must have "off-time." By having this, they can get re-energized and be actively involved with their families, with friends, and with their communities. Hence, "emotional balancing" is vitally important. Such a practice involves managing the emotional needs of change agents and change recipients. At the organizational level, it brings to the fore the engagement and commitment of change agents so as to energize change programs. It also necessitates middle managers recognizing the emotional needs of the people they are responsible for. The aforementioned must come about in order to sustain work-life integration and positive work-life dynamics, as well as high quality client/business relations. These needs must be met to continue employee and company development and to ensure positive acceptance of new knowledge and skills (Huy, 2002). It must be recognized, moreover, that in the absence of "emotional balancing," in the turmoil of change, that rather than the enterprise's new strategic transformation effort, employees may feel fatigued, and more concerned about their own health and well-being (think: constant tiredness, insomnia, muscular tensions, migraine headaches, appetite issues, and other symptoms).

Part 2

If organizational performance is mediocre or if significant parts of it are misaligned with regard to strategy, structure, processes and lateral capability, incentives, the pay system, resources, learning and talent development practices, this issue must be subject to re-construction through "redesign." Still, "moving" *à la* Lewin (Step 2), i.e., "transforming" into new behaviors, may not be successful. This is especially so when large-scale, system-wide organizational restructuring is frantically undertaken so as to cope with hyper-competitive environments, even though the "unfrozen" organization is not exactly "healthy" or "energized."

Furthermore, "rebalancing" *à la* Weick (Step 2), i.e., removing blockages in adaptive processes, might not generate spectacular results either, as "sensemaking" alone cannot control reorganization so as to gain greater efficiency. Leaders by themselves also cannot manage the change recipients' schemata effectively (especially in virtual global organizations) if the recipients are largely unaware of the goals. In addition, outdated or conflicting cognitive representations, meanings, images, and interpretations of the same rebalancing actions can exist within the same organization. Among these are the change leaders' frames of conceptual change being wholly different to the employees' competing mental representations of the same interventions.

All of the previous may actually immobilize the affected change parties. As a result, desired outcomes are often not achieved. Because of this, "redesigning," taking into account the type and scale of change, may mean systematic remodeling, or redesigning organizational structure, business practices and policies to support the advancement of change. Thus, nowadays, leaders need to fully understand what designers are trying to bring about. Moreover, in leading positive strategic change, change leaders must also be organizational "change designers" or social architects of their organizations, themselves, and think "design". Design thinking (DT), evidently, is revolutionary – it is effectively a new competitive tool (Brown, 2009; *DMI Review*, 2011; Martin, 2009).

In the real world, "redesigning" implies using the designer's sensibility. It means using design-centric methods such as visioning to co-craft the positive in strategic collaboration with organizational members and stakeholders by way of collective thinking. It is also undertaking an appreciative future search by asking *What is already working well? What if anything were possible? What wows? What happens to that, if we do this?*. Furthermore, it means analyzing strengths-opportunities-aspirations-results (SOAR), mapping change journeys, out-imagining and reframing problems. In addition, it implies co-creating, rapid prototyping and testing, iterating, strategizing as a design process, and proactively running a series of disciplined learning launches so as to de-risk the change initiative execution.

Thus, in order to accelerate change, simplify work processes, uncover more insights, rapidly respond to difficult situations, and update staff on redesign efforts in real time, "redesigning" should incorporate digital tool usage. Among these are visually immersive "just-in-time" data systems, such as shared "heat maps," for decision-making, and personalized messaging systems, such as instant feedback messaging, private social networks, and wearable technology. Such tools help personnel to collaborate across geographic space, to learn from each other and from clients, to engage and enhance the inter-staff and customer experience.

Part 3

Rather than "freezing" (Lewin's Step 3) – something too "solid" for the super-dynamic times of today, or further "unfreezing" (Weick's Step 3), which could be, in reality, disruptive to an established healthy system, change leaders can choose to "gel." "Gelling," in terms of dynamic organizational capability, implies bringing about a *"semi*-solid" state. A state such as this is solid enough to ensure that the newly "crystalized" status quo is safe from regression to old behaviors and performances, while it simultaneously enables examination and positive modification. Furthermore, it makes allowance for strategic agility, adaptability, recreating, and reinventing; strategic agility is understood as "the ability to remain flexible in facing new developments, to continuously adjust the company's strategic direction, and to develop innovative ways to create value" (Weber & Tarba, 2014: 5).

In today's enterprises, many business leaders have to drive a continuous organizing process to achieve enough flexibility to get on with the business while also inventing new business. "Gelling" empowers the organization to flexibly take hold of opportunities that arise through positive hyperdynamic change while withstanding punctuated equilibrium, "tectonic" or "cataclysmic" shocks. Hence, it gives the corporate entity a form of strategic *super-flexibility* (Bahrami & Evans, 2010; 2011). When "gelling," change managers should be constantly modeling, monitoring, measuring, and reflecting upon the ongoing performance and outcomes of change across the firm and making use of insights obtained. All such decisions that arise through "gelling" must be based on evidence, with the metrics chosen in an open-book way. Moreover, the change lessons learned must be integrated and the resulting know-how must be transferred. In addition, the obtained momentum must be reinforced and sustained so as to keep strategizing to win. Finally, positive corporate regeneration must be near-continuous and enabled by analysis and (re)design, experimentation, (open) innovation, learning and development. After all, change is *managed* learning.

Converging areas of research that inform ERG

The proposed organization development and change process consists of three positive strategic change phases (energize, redesign, gel), and 15 associated dynamic actions (see Table 1.3 for a complete design). This is all the outgrowth of three newly emerging areas of research. The first of these is Positive Organizational Scholarship (POS) (Cameron *et al.*, 2003; Cameron & Spreitzer, 2012). The second is Design Thinking (DT) (Austin & Devin, 2003; Boland & Collopy, 2004; *CMR*, 2020; *DMI Review*, 2015; Martin, 2009). The third is Organizational Ambidexterity – particularly Super-Flexibility (Bahrami & Evans, 2010; 2011).

First, POS, a new and exciting movement in organization studies, primarily focuses on "the study of especially the positive outcomes, processes, and attributes of organizations and their members" (Cameron *et al.*, 2003: 4). Here, *positive* organizational change is led in accordance with strategic intent and organizational purpose. This intent is to bring about a crafted positive future state wherein "the positive" is emphasized. Such positives include positive organizational development, organizational energy, generative dynamics, resource mobilizing, and strengths finding. These positives also bring into the fold evangelizing the change purpose, positive socialization

Table 1.3 Positive organizational change: Energize, redesign, gel (ERG)

Positive strategic change phases of the continuing cycle	*Dynamic actions*
1. Energize	• Diagnose for change, including undertaking a pre-change audit of the system-wide fitness for organizational change, as well as an inquiry into organizational memory, and experience of past change initiatives • Awaken by building a compelling case for change, as well as by evangelizing the change purpose, touching and connecting with people by means of storytelling and collaborative and generative "change conversations" • Mobilize resources and find strengths • Select and engage positive culture-fit "change energizers" • Socialize and empathize with others and with the workplace environment as a whole
2. Redesign	• Co-craft the "sunnier side of life" in strategic collaboration with organizational members and stakeholders, by way of collective design thinking and appreciative future search (*What is already working well? What if anything were possible? What exactly wows? What happens to that, if we do this?*) • Remodel organizational structure, processes, and components, if necessary • Navigate and manage power and politics, resistance, a change coalition (e.g. a dedicated "design team"), and core business • Coach and develop for positive leadership, engagement, and organizational renewal • Before roll-out, run disciplined learning launches – to de-risk change initiative execution
3. Gel	• Continuously model, monitor, and measure progress and performance – basing decisions upon metrics chosen in an open book way • Reward and celebrate quick wins • Integrate change lessons learned • Reinforce and sustain the organization's new state • Keep strategizing to win, and keep self-regenerating through continuous, experiential, social and reflective learning, self-organizing, designing, experimenting, and innovating (including practicing open innovation via crowdsourcing, innovation intermediaries, or open innovation software)

and positive workplace culture-fit, the provision of opportunities to play and have "meaningful fun." In addition, the "sunnier side of life" is co-created, positive communication is established, and continuous learning and development for positive leadership are emphasized. Finally, POS must include reward and the celebration of success.

POS skeptics point out the overemphasis on positive values – with *positive* being undefined, and they especially note that POS neglects the *negative* (Fineman, 2006; George, 2004). It is true that POS, conceptually, is not value-neutral.

However, current business-related literature provides many connotations of "positive," for example, "positive" represents *positive alternative*. Hence, it can be said that the problems that arise in reconstruction are, in POS, construed as opportunities and strength-developing incidents (Gittell *et al.*, 2006).

In POS, certain variables and generative dynamics come to be fundamental. Included among these are "positive human and organizational energy" (Baker *et al.*, 2003; Bruch & Ghoshal, 2003; Bruch & Vogel, 2011; Carmeli *et al.*, 2009; Cross *et al.*, 2003; Dutton, 2003a; Gratton, 2007; Schwartz, 2007), and "positive organizational behavior" (POB) (Luthans, 2002a; 2002b), particularly "psychological capital" (PsyCap). This is comprised of optimism, hope, confidence, and resiliency. These all are positively oriented psychological capacities that can be measured, developed, and effectively managed for performance improvement (Luthans *et al.*, 2007a; Luthans *et al.*, 2007b; Peterson *et al.*, 2008).

These variables and dynamics also include "appreciative inquiry" – a narrative-based process of search and discovery of what gives life to an enterprise or a community (Cooperrider *et al.*, 2003; Cooperrider & Whitney, 2005). Assimilation also comes about by means of building "resilience" and finding meaning in the face of adversity (Sandberg & Grant, 2017), "organizational healing" being considered a relational process to counter major disruptions (Powley, 2012), embracing "biophilic work design" mostly for the purpose of employee well-being and sustainability (Klotz, 2020), "sustainable return to work" (Nielsen et al., 2018), and job redesign, by means of employee-centered "job crafting" wherein employees, being active crafters of their work, make the job fit them, rather than them attempting to fit themselves to the job (Wrzesniewski *et al.*, 2010; Wrzesniewski & Dutton, 2001). The dynamics of POS also incorporates "thriving" at work (Carmeli & Spreitzer, 2009; Spreitzer *et al.*, 2005), "connectivity" (Dutton, 2003b; Losada & Heaphy, 2004), and "positive group affect spiral" (Walter & Bruch, 2008). The latter is a positive affective mechanism that is supported by emerging neuroscientific evidence (Bagozzi & Verbeke, 2012; Cattaneo & Rizzolatti, 2009; Iacoboni, 2009).

What is more, "positive" incorporates *dynamic capability building* and *a resource-based* orientation. It taps into the human resources that teams and companies need so as to renew, capitalize upon, and build up capabilities and strengths (Clifton & Harter, 2003). "Positive" also embraces *dynamic capabilities* – this being "the capacity of an organization to purposefully create, extend, or modify its resource base" (Helfat *et al.*, 2007: 4).

Ultimately, "positive" refers to POS in *positively deviant performance*, i.e., extraordinary effectiveness, spectacular results, and performance *far* above the norm (Cameron, 2008; Cameron & Lavine, 2006; Spreitzer & Sonenshein, 2003). Therefore, in practice, POS accentuates the positive, rather than ignoring the negative – what was done right, rather than what was done wrong. It is also open to applying much more than just limited deficit-based approaches to problem solving (Caza & Cameron, 2008; Roberts, 2006).

In the next place, Design Thinking (DT) (Austin & Devin, 2003; Boland & Collopy, 2004; *CMR*, 2020; *DMI Review*, 2015; Martin, 2009) is considered to be an effective step-wise enabler-identifying and purpose-finding method. It involves an attitude of open inquiry, visioning, liberating the entrepreneurial spirit and energy of the workforce, which they can then use to introduce new products and services and otherwise improve things, co-creating organizational change with customers, experience journey mapping, using empathy exercises, observing behaviors in context and often engaging with "extreme" users, building positive future scenarios, as well as reframing issues, ideating/iterating and strategizing as a design process. DT embraces "thinking *and* doing." Hence, in order to remove the risk from the change initiative execution, disciplined learning launches are run to see if mock-ups meet the reality. Ultimately, good design is good for everybody.

These actions are critical to those wishing to embrace deep insight, and, hence, to think strategically, in order to counter the complexity of change, and to deliver value through (re)design and innovation. Emphasis is placed upon big ideas and on development through organic radical innovation. Although the DT movement is relatively new, it should be noted that design-driven companies such as Apple, Coca-Cola, Ford, Herman-Miller, IBM, Intuit, Newell-Rubbermaid, Nike, P&G, Starbucks, Starwood, Steelcase, Target, Walt Disney, and Whirlpool have outperformed the Standard & Poor's 500, a stock market index of 500 large publicly traded companies, by an extraordinary 228 percent (Westcott, 2014).

Last but not least, corporate entities must be efficient in their management of today's business, and adaptable in order to cope with tomorrow's changing demands. "Super-flexibility" is "the capacity to thrive on fluid reality and adjust to morphing conditions" (Bahrami & Evans, 2011: 24). Practically, as enterprises are forced into ever more and more frequent cycles of reorganizing and strategizing, "super-flexibility" means

> engaging in a delicate balancing act: deciding what to keep and how to stay the course on the one hand, and thinking about where and how to make swift and sudden changes to capitalize on new realities, on the other hand. In a nutshell, super-flexibility refers to the dialectical capacity of withstanding while transforming.
>
> (Bahrami & Evans, 2011: 24)

In grasping the big picture, what needs underlining is the fact that change is a continuous process in which all of the framework steps and activity influence and reinforce one another. In the proposed playbook, ERG change stages are iterative and continuous and if one stage is left out, the transformation will fail. The order of concrete dynamic actions within the stages is not dogmatic (unlike in some *n*-step change models). Therefore, the actions cataloged below may or may not be followed sequentially and can vary, depending on the change situation (type, timing, stage, and depth – how far it penetrates the firm). As change is "messy" and full of surprises, it is up to the change leader to skillfully adapt this model to their specific change situation and unique organizational setting.

Conclusion

The aforementioned discussion reflects a deeper understanding of what today's organization development (OD) and change management are and are not. In viewing OD and change through the lens of *"positive* organizational," "design," and "super-flexibility" perspectives, one sees this strategic process anew, in more color and depth, and in doing so, it is evident that there is a need to challenge many received dogmas. OD and change from a *positive* organizational/design/super-flexibility perspective, as advanced in this book, are not like OD and change from a *positive* organizational/design/super-flexibility-*free* perspective.

Seeing that never-ending change is now the norm, that all enterprises are in flux and that change is accelerating, to undertake successful strategic transformations that deliver and sustain enhanced performance, organizations need to change the way they change. They need to reinvent themselves and learn to remake themselves into more energized, design-driven, and super-flexible enterprises. By all means, driving effective change can be frustrating, yet, it can be done.

The intent of this chapter is to demystify change. It champions a simple and powerful framework for progressive thinking through organizational change and renewal. It also puts forward a shared language for thinking about change within an enterprise, and it offers a playbook for executing transformations – strategically *and* positively. Basically, the new positive OD and change process consists of three positive strategic change phases (energize, redesign, gel) and 15 associated dynamic actions.

As survival, health and thriving rest on continuous positive change, being always change-ready and not just episodically ready, is crucial in designing and building *change-able* organizations. These enterprises can adapt freely so as to build and sustain sure-footed adaptability advantage and be one step ahead of the game. This means shifting to a positive strategic transformation mindset and developing a positive culture that is energized by change, and has an identity built around it. What is more, it is a culture in which all employees treat change as a continuum, as a norm, rather than a one-time effort, specific target, or a massive enterprise earthquake – a complete surprise.

It must be emphasized that rigid change programs crafted at boardroom level only, without company-wide change dialog and positive input from those at the front line who are directly affected by the change, are doomed to failure.

Beyond everything, leading change means employing *positive collective* leadership, namely, making sure that everybody understands the new strategy, direction, and winning aspirations, and can purposefully relate it to his or her own area of work. Success in achieving the necessary energizing, redesigning, and gelling that such change calls for is essential, because, in the present climate, enterprises have relatively short periods in which they can keep a competitive edge before their strategic assets become rather irrelevant.

Summary propositions

Recap and revise the key takeaways from this chapter:

- This chapter demystifies change. Managing organizational change can be "messy" and full of surprises – there are forces for stability and forces pushing for change. Yet, it is doable. Fundamentally, leading change combines rigor *and* creativity.
- Two classic three-step change management models are reviewed and critiqued.
- An alternative model of *positive* organizational change is put forward. The new playbook for change is composed of three "positive strategic change phases" (energize, redesign, and gel) and 15 related "dynamic actions" that should be cycled through, when changing the organization for the better. ERG is a cycle of action and learning over time that leads to sustained and beneficial change.
- Notions emphasized are the "positive" (energizing the workplace, enhancing organizational health and renewal), "design" (putting into place collective design thinking and appreciative future search), and "organizational ambidexterity" (thriving on fluid reality and adapting to change super-flexibly), so as to bring forth a golden future for, and health and prosperity within the organization.
- Of note is the fact that *positive* dynamics (like relational energy, strengths, trust, organizational forgiveness, optimism, virtue, and so on) that bring about positive effects in individuals, teams, groups, and enterprises (such as improved performance and productivity or heightened organizational learning) do not ignore the *negative*. Rather, the positive approach completes and expands the perspective of those who constantly zoom in on what goes wrong.
- Increasingly, executive leadership teams are thrown into VUCA chaos – characterized by *volatility, uncertainty, complexity,* and *ambiguity* (think: strategic changes, epidemics and pandemics, paradigm shifts, new ways of doing business and working, economic decline, disruptive innovation, technological change, downsizing, mergers, or managing the rise of the virtual workplace). In fact, there is nowhere to turn to get away from the VUCA world. Therefore, being *continuously change-ready*, and not just episodically ready, is essential today – this helps build renewal capabilities, organizational capacity, and adaptability for the future. The ERG model empowers *learning-ready* organizations operating in turbulent environments to anticipate change and to constantly reconfigure and to successfully deliver change and performance – performance far above the norm.

Acknowledgments

An earlier and shorter version of this chapter was published as "A Playbook for Positive Organizational Change: Energize, Redesign, and Gel," by B. Tkaczyk, in *Strategic Change* 24(6), 2015, in a Special Issue on New Strategies for Innovative Performance. Copyright © 2015, John Wiley & Sons Ltd. The author is grateful to the publisher of the journal for granting the right to republish the article. Also, the author thanks Carlo Milana for his helpful comments on an earlier version.

References for further reading

Ackenhusen, M., Muzyka, D., & Churchill N. (1996). Restructuring 3M for an integrated Europe. Part one: Initiating the change. *European Management Journal*, 14(1), 21–36.

Agarwal, N., & Kwan, P. (2018). Pricing mergers with differential synergies. *Strategic Change*, 27(1), 3–7.

Agarwal, N., Kwan, P., & Paul, D. (2018). Behavioral merger and acquisition pricing: Application to Verizon mergers with AOL and Yahoo. *Strategic Change*, 27(1), 9–21.

Agrawal, A., Gans, J., & Goldfarb, A. (2018). *Prediction machines: The simple economics of artificial intelligence.* Boston, MA: Harvard Business Review Press.

ASTD. (2013). *Virtual leadership: Going the distance to manage your teams.* Alexandria, VA: The American Society for Training and Development.

ASTD. (2014). *Change agents: The role of organizational learning in change management.* Alexandria, VA: The American Society for Training and Development.

Austin, R., & Devin, L. (2003). *Artful making: What managers need to know about how artists work.* Upper Saddle River, NJ: Financial Times Prentice Hall.

Bagozzi, R., & Verbeke, W. (2012). The neuroscience underpinning of POS. Exploring the minds of managers: Insights from three neuroscience studies. In K. Cameron & G. Spreitzer (Eds.), *Oxford handbook of positive organizational scholarship* (pp. 138–151). New York, NY: Oxford University Press.

Bahrami, H., & Evans, S. (2010). *Super-flexibility for knowledge enterprises: A toolkit for dynamic adaptation.* Heidelberg, Germany: Springer.

Bahrami, H., & Evans, S. (2011). Super-flexibility for real-time adaptation: Perspectives from Silicon Valley. *California Management Review*, 53(3), 21–39.

Baker, W. (2004). Half-baked brown bag presentation on positive energy networks. Unpublished manuscript, University of Michigan Business School.

Baker, W., Cross, R., & Wooten, M. (2003). Positive organizational network analysis and energizing relationships. In K. Cameron, J. Dutton, & R. Quinn (Eds.), *Positive organizational scholarship: Foundations of a new discipline* (pp. 328–342). San Francisco, CA: Berrett-Koehler Publishers.

Boland, R., & Collopy, F. (Eds.). (2004). *Managing as designing.* Stanford, CA: Stanford University Press.

Boudreau, J., & Rice, S. (2015). Bright, shiny objects and the future of HR. How Juniper Networks tests and integrates the most valuable new approaches. *Harvard Business Review*, 93(7), 72–78.

Brown, T. (2009). *Change by design: How design thinking transforms organizations and inspires innovation.* New York, NY: HarperBusiness.

Bruch, H., & Ghoshal, S. (2003). Unleashing organizational energy. *MIT Sloan Management Review*, 45(1), 45–51.

Bruch, H., & Vogel, B. (2011). *Fully-charged: How great leaders boost their organization's energy and ignite high performance*. Boston, MA: Harvard Business Review Press.

Cameron, K. (2008). *Positive leadership: Strategies for extraordinary performance*. San Francisco, CA: Berrett-Koehler Publishers.

Cameron, K., Dutton, J., & Quinn, R. (Eds.). (2003). *Positive organizational scholarship: Foundations of a new discipline*. San Francisco, CA: Berrett-Koehler Publishers.

Cameron, K., & Lavine, M. (2006). *Making the impossible possible: Leading extraordinary performance – The Rocky Flats story*. San Francisco, CA: Berrett-Koehler Publishers.

Cameron, K., & Spreitzer, G. (Eds.). (2012). *The Oxford handbook of positive organizational scholarship*. New York, NY: Oxford University Press.

Carmeli, A., Ben-Hador, B., Waldman, D., & Rupp, D. (2009). How leaders cultivate social capital and nurture employee vigor: Implications for job performance. *Journal of Applied Psychology*, 94(6), 1553–1561.

Carmeli, A., & Spreitzer, G. (2009). Trust, connectivity, and thriving: Implications for innovative behaviors at work. *The Journal of Creative Behavior*, 43(3), 169–191.

Cascio, W. (1993). Downsizing: what do we know? What have we learned? *Academy of Management Executive*, 7(1), 95–104.

Cascio, W. (2002). Strategies for responsible restructuring. *Academy of Management Executive*, 16(3), 80–91.

Cascio, W., Chatrath, A., & Christie-David, R.A. (2020). Antecedents and consequences of employment and asset restructuring. *Academy of Management Journal*. Retrieved from: https://journals.aom.org/doi/10.5465/amj.2018.1013

Cattaneo, L., & Rizzolatti, G. (2009). The mirror neuron system. *Neurobiological Review*, 66(5), 557–560.

Caza, A., & Cameron, K. (2008). Positive organizational scholarship: What does it achieve? In C. L. Cooper & S. R. Clegg (Eds.), *The Sage handbook of organizational behavior: Macro approaches* (vol. 2, pp. 99–116). New York, NY: Sage Publications.

Cennamo, C., Dagnino, G. B., Di Minin, A., & Lanzolla, G. (2020). Managing digital transformation: Scope of transformation and modalities of value co-generation and delivery. *California Management Review*, 62(4), 5–16.

Clifton, D., & Harter, J. (2003). Investing in strengths. In K. Cameron, J. Dutton, & R. Quinn (Eds.), *Positive organizational scholarship: Foundations of a new discipline* (pp. 111–121). San Francisco, CA: Berrett-Koehler Publishers.

CMR. (2020). Special issue on design thinking. *California Management Review*, 62(2).

Cooperrider, D., & Whitney, D. (2005). *Appreciative inquiry: A positive revolution in change*. San Francisco, CA: Berrett-Koehler Publishers.

Cooperrider, D., Whitney, D., & Stavros, J. (2003). *Appreciative inquiry handbook*. Bedford Heights, OH: Lakeshore Publishers.

Crisp, G., Bonello, C., Zimmerman, J., & Olarte, T. (2018). Leadership forum: Making digital transformation a reality. *Rotman Management*, Winter, 52–55.

Cross, R., Baker, W., & Parker, A. (2003). What creates energy in organizations? *MIT Sloan Management Review*, 44(4), 51–56.

Denning, S. (2011, October 31). Steve Jobs: Management innovator. *Forbes*.

DMI Review. (2011). Design management metrics: Assessing quality and outcomes. *DMI Review,* 22(2).

DMI Review. (2015). Organization development and design management. *DMI Review,* 26(3).

Dutton, J. (2003a). *Energize your workplace: How to create and sustain high-quality connections at work.* San Francisco, CA: Jossey-Bass.

Dutton, J. (2003b). Fostering high quality connections through respectful engagement. *Stanford Social Innovation Review,* Winter, 54–57.

Edelman. (2019). 2019 Edelman trust barometer (Global report). Daniel J. Edelman Holdings, Inc. Retrieved from: www.edelman.com/sites/g/files/aatuss191/files/2019-02/2019_Edelman_Trust_Barometer_Global_Report.pdf

Feld, C., & Stoddard, D. (2004). Getting IT right. *Harvard Business Review,* 82(2), 72–79.

Fineman, S. (2006). On being positive: Concerns and counterpoints. *Academy of Management Review,* 31(2), 270–291.

George, J. M. (2004). Positive organizational scholarship: Foundations of a new discipline. *Administrative Science Quarterly,* 49(2), 325–330.

Gerdeman, D. (2020, March 16). How the coronavirus is already rewriting the future of business. *Harvard Business School Working Knowledge (HBSWK).*

Ghoshal, S., & Bartlett, C. (1996). Rebuilding behavioral context: A blueprint for corporate renewal. *MIT Sloan Management Review,* 37(2), 23–36.

Gittell, J., Cameron, K., Lim, S., & Rivas, V. (2006), Relationships, layoffs, and organizational resilience. *Journal of Applied Behavioral Science,* 42(3), 300–329.

Gomes, E. (2020). Mergers, acquisitions, and strategic alliances as collaborative methods of strategic development and change. *Strategic Change,* 29(2), 145–148.

Gomes, E., Alam, S., Tarba, S. Y., & Vendrell-Herrero, F. (2020). A 27-year review of mergers and acquisitions research in 27 leading management journals. *Strategic Change,* 29(2), 179–193.

Gratton, L. (2007). *Hot spots: Why some companies buzz with energy and innovation – and others don't.* Harlow, UK: Financial Times Prentice Hall.

Gratton, L., & Scott, A. (2016). *The 100-year life: Living and working in an age of longevity.* London, UK: Bloomsbury Information.

Greising, D. (2001, September 9). True confession: Boeing among GE copycats. *Chicago Tribune.*

Grove, A. (1999). *Only the paranoid survive: How to exploit the crisis points that challenge every company.* New York, NY: Crown Business.

HBR. (2011). *HBR's 10 must reads on change.* Boston, MA: Harvard Business Review Press.

Helfat, C., Finkelstein, S., Mitchell, W., Peteraf, M., Singh, H., Teece, D., & Winter, S. (2007). *Dynamic capabilities: Understanding strategic change in organizations.* Malden, MA: Blackwell Publishing.

HMD. (2007). *Human mortality database.* University of California, Berkeley, and Max Planck Institute for Demographic Research, Germany. Retrieved from: www.mortality.org

Hotten, R. (2015, December 10). Volkswagen: The scandal explained. *BBC News.*

Huy, Q. (2002). Emotional balancing of organizational continuity and radical change: The contribution of middle managers. *Administrative Science Quarterly,* 47(1), 31–69.

Iacoboni, M. (2009). Imitation, empathy, and mirror neurons. *Annual Review of Psychology,* 60, 653–670.

Johnson, C. (2018, January 30). Amazon, Berkshire Hathaway and JP Morgan Chase join forces to tackle employees' health-care costs. *Washington Post.*

Jordan, M., & Stuart, N. (2000). Lessons learned. *CMA Management,* 74(3), 35.

Kirkpatrick, D. (2006, September 5). Dell in the penalty box. *Fortune.*

Klotz, A. (2020). Creating jobs and workspaces that energize people. *MIT Sloan Management Review,* 61(4), 74–78.

Lewin, K. (1947). Frontiers in group dynamics. *Human Relations,* 1(1), 5–41.

Losada, M., & Heaphy, E. (2004). The role of positivity and connectivity in the performance of business teams: A nonlinear dynamics model. *American Behavioral Scientist,* 47(6), 740–765.

Luthans, F. (2002a). The need for and meaning of positive organizational behavior. *Journal of Organizational Behavior,* 23(6), 695–706.

Luthans, F. (2002b). Positive organizational behavior: Developing and managing psychological strengths. *Academy of Management Executive,* 16(1), 57–72.

Luthans, F., Avolio, B., Avey, J., & Norman, S. (2007a). Positive psychological capital: Measurement and relationship with performance and satisfaction. *Personnel Psychology,* 60(3), 541–572.

Luthans, F., Youssef, C., & Avolio, B. (2007b). *Psychological capital: Developing the human competitive edge.* Oxford, UK: Oxford University Press.

Martin, R. (2009). *The design of business: Why design thinking is the next competitive advantage.* Boston, MA: Harvard Business Press.

Mickle, T. (2020, February 17). Apple to fall short of projected revenue due to coronavirus. *The Wall Street Journal.*

Millar, C., Groth, O., & Mahon, J. (2018). Management innovation in a VUCA world: Challenges and recommendations. *California Management Review,* 61(1), 5–14.

MIT. (2020). *How AI changes the rules: New imperatives for the intelligent organization.* Boston, MA: Massachusetts Institute of Technology.

Mulligan, T., & Kraul, C. (1996, November 16). Texaco settles race bias suit for $176 million. *Los Angeles Times.*

Nielsen. (2014). *Doing well by doing good.* New York, NY: The Nielsen Company.

Nielsen, K., Yarker, J., Munir F., & Bültmann, U. (2018). Igloo: An integrated framework for sustainable return to work in workers with common mental disorders. *Work & Stress,* 32(4), 400–417.

Nooyi, I. K., & Govindarajan, V. (2020). Becoming a better corporate citizen: How PepsiCo moved toward a healthier future. *Harvard Business Review,* 98(2), 94–103.

Olson, M. L. (2008). Compact risk: Controlling the perils of change. *T+D,* 62(9), 38–43.

Peterson, S., Balthazard, P., Waldman, D., & Thatcher, R. (2008). Neuroscientific implications of psychological capital: Are the brains of optimistic, hopeful, confident, and resilient leaders different? *Organizational Dynamics,* 37(4), 342–353.

Powley, E. (2012). Organizational healing: A relational process to handle major disruption. In K. Cameron & G. Spreitzer (Eds.), *Oxford handbook of positive organizational scholarship* (pp. 855–866). New York, NY: Oxford University Press.

Reeves, M., Fæste, L., Whitaker, K., & Hassan, F. (2018). The truth about corporate transformation. *MIT Sloan Management Review.* Retrieved from: http://mitsmr.com/2DQSmF4

Roberts, L. (2006). Shifting the lens on organizational life: The added value of positive scholarship. *Academy of Management Review,* 31(2), 292–305.

Sandberg, S., & Grant, A. (2017). *Option B: Facing adversity, building resilience, and finding joy.* New York, NY: Knopf.

Schwartz, T. (2007). Manage your energy, not your time. *Harvard Business Review*, 85(10), 63–73.

Sellers, P. (1997, April 28). Sears: The turnaround is ending. *Fortune.*

Spreitzer, G., & Sonenshein, S. (2003). Positive deviance and extraordinary organizing. In K. Cameron, J. Dutton, & R. Quinn (Eds.), *Positive organizational scholarship: Foundations of a new discipline* (pp. 207–224). San Francisco, CA: Berrett-Koehler Publishers.

Spreitzer, G., Sutcliffe, K., Dutton, J., Sonenshein, S., & Grant, A. (2005). A socially embedded model of thriving at work. *Organization Science*, 16(5), 537–549.

Tkaczyk, B. (2014a). Daily check-ins stimulate self-improvement. *Talent Development (TD)*, 68(8), 72–73.

Tkaczyk, B. (2014b). Crafting continuing learning and development: A positive design tool for leadership development. *Development and Learning in Organizations: An International Journal*, 28(4), 5–8.

Tushman, M., & O'Reilly C III. (1996). Ambidextrous organizations: Managing evolutionary and revolutionary change. *California Management Review*, 38(4), 8–30.

UN. (2015). *The sustainable development goals.* New York, NY: The United Nations. Retrieved from: www.un.org/sustainabledevelopment/sustainable-development-goals/

Walter, F., & Bruch, H. (2008). The positive group affect spiral: A dynamic model of the emergence of positive affective similarity in work groups. *Journal of Organizational Behavior*, 29(2), 239–261.

Weber, Y., & Tarba, S. Y. (2014). Strategic agility: A state of the art. *California Management Review*, 56(3), 5–12.

Weber, Y., Tarba, S. Y., & Oberg, C. (2014). *A comprehensive guide to mergers & acquisitions.* Upper Saddle River, NJ: FT Press.

Weick, K. (1995). *Sensemaking in organizations.* Thousand Oaks, CA: Sage Publications.

Weick, K. (2000). Emergent change as a universal in organizations. In M. Beer & N. Nohira (Eds.), *Breaking the code of change* (pp. 223–241). Boston, MA: Harvard Business School Press.

Weick, K., Sutcliffe, K., & Obstfeld, D. (2005). Organizing and the process of sensemaking. *Organization Science*, 16(4), 409–451.

Weill, P., & Woerner, S.L. (2018). Is your company ready for a digital future? *MIT Sloan Management Review*, 59(2), 21–25.

Westcott, M. (2014). Design-driven companies outperform S&P by 228% over 10 years – the 'DMI design value index.' *Design Management Institute: Dialog.* Retrieved from: www.dmi.org/blogpost/1093220/182956/Design-Driven-Companies-Outperform-S-P-by-228-Over-Ten-Years--The-DMI-Design-Value-Index

Wrzesniewski, A., Berg, J., & Dutton, J. (2010). Turn the job you have into the job you want. *Harvard Business Review*, 88(6), 114–117.

Wrzesniewski, A., & Dutton, J. (2001). Crafting a job: Revisioning employees as active crafters of their work. *Academy of Management Review*, 26(2), 179–201.

Yoder, E. (1998). Mint condition. *Government Executive*, 30(9), 51–56.

Zhao, Y. (2002, December 29). Verizon layoffs leave 246 worried. *The New York Times.*

2 Team coaching for *positive* organizational change

Building and sustaining high-quality teams via ERG

Lead-in

Professional coaching, one of the fastest-growing professions in the world, helps talented individuals and teams to achieve their personal and professional best. Coaching task-performing executive leadership teams (ELTs) for change management is different from coaching individuals. Team coaching is not a mysterious solo act, and it is not a substitute for individual coaching either. Rather, it is a complementary method. In a world that is increasingly aware of the power of teams inside and outside organizations, team-centered coaching should be highlighted in the learning and development (L&D) portfolios of enterprises in order to nurture top team development and organization effectiveness and health. Team-focused coaching, grounded in dialogic Organization Development (OD) and behavioral science, is an ideal mechanism for accelerating and sustaining change. Making use of generative coaching conversations around change issues helps organizations to strategize more openly, and to create new awareness, behaviors, possibilities, and outcomes – to collaboratively create that new future. Getting from dilemma to solution is strategic, requiring imaginative responses within a team-based coaching methodology built on team agreement; a cycle of energizing, redesigning, and gelling; and a dialogic approach to learning.

Dialogic reflection for professional team development

In your team, discuss the following questions:

1. Are your team meetings compelling and productive? Why are so many teams dysfunctional?
2. In your organization, do senior executives play together as a team while also leading their own functions – all in harmony? What does it take to make executive leadership teams great? How to set the team up correctly

so that these high-powered senior leaders pull together to move the organization forward?

3. What do you think about executive coaching for change management and engagement delivered as a series of *one-to-one* conversations?
4. Are you familiar with some effective solution-focused techniques that can be applied in an executive leadership *team* environment? Does your organization have a robust culture of *dialogic* organization development and team-centered coaching in place? Do you think team coaching could help team-based problem-solving?
5. "Change starts with changing everyday conversations." Do you agree or disagree with this statement?
6. How can enterprises promote best-team functioning by using positive team climate approaches?
7. What is the best way to build collaborative behaviors and develop teams that will be adaptable to future change as enterprises are forced into ever more frequent cycles of strategizing and reorganizing?
8. How can a productive balance of cohesion and adaptability in teams be created in an enterprise going through some disruptive change?
9. Now, reflect upon your own function. How far do you see the function to be working in a silo, or, on the other hand, to be cutting across all internal boundaries and reaching out across the external – in order to co-create value throughout the value chain of your business?
10. "All organizations can learn, relearn, and unlearn." Do you agree or disagree with this statement?

Everybody needs a coach.

(Eric Schmidt, former Google CEO)

The specific approach to change embraced in this book helps one to appreciate *change-able* organizations as super-flexible (able to achieve the performance targets of the existing business, while navigating chaos and reinventing themselves); as self-organizing (to achieve an equilibrium); as networked (interacting with dynamic environments in complex ways–and even thriving on complexity); and as buzzing with positive energy, continuous learning-based process improvement, as well as organic radical innovation. In such organizations, everyone is talented, and organizational learning is rooted in culture. To tell the truth, *strategic* organizational learning is the heart of any productive activity – it is the trending form of labor. Indeed, over the long run, superior organizational performance relies on superior organizational learning. Specifically, know-how assets embedded in routines, and effective organizational learning undergird dynamic capabilities, and these in turn help top performers to retain the competitive edge (Tkaczyk, 2015).

Unleashing the potential for change has become the Holy Grail. This can be done via *dialogic* Organization Development – herein, a change leader facilitates processes that make use of generative coaching conversations around change issues to strategize more openly, and to create new awareness, behaviors, capabilities, possibilities, and outcomes – to create that new future.

The change leader as coach: coaching is not just for problems anymore

Professional coaching, one of the fastest-growing professions world-wide, aids individuals and teams to be at their personal and professional best. Rather than train people, a coach energizes and equips talented and resourceful people to develop themselves and to maximize their own potential. Evidently, coaching can help successful people change enormously (Goldsmith, 2003). Excellent change leadership involves a synergistic com-bination of agentic skills (e.g., getting the work done) and people skills (e.g., using positive communication). A substantial set of skills is brought to this task by such coaches. These include an ability to set the stage and help de-fine the "moonshot" goals; bring to the fore a positive leadership presence; ask penetrating and appropriate questions, and actively listen – with nuance and sensitivity, track and challenge responses in a non-hostile manner; give and receive actionable feedback; inspire with positive inquiry; establish the highest levels of trust, openness, and high-quality connection – develop the "human chemistry" needed to be successful.

"Everybody needs a coach," according to Google giant, Eric Schmidt, and every team can benefit from a coach who understands that *team*-focused coaching is more than coaching in multiples. *Individual* coaching is now wholly recognized as a useful learning and development (L&D) method, but coaching task-performing executive teams is neither well established nor un-derstood. Team coaching is not a matter of collectively coaching a set of in-dependent individuals; it is a sophisticated process of coaching a system of interdependent persons that must build synergistically to achieve a shared outcome. Team-centered coaching, when done well, fuels and strengthens a team's performance, engendering maximum effectiveness. Grounded in *dialogic* OD and *behavioral* science, team-based coaching is an ideal mecha-nism for accelerating and sustaining change.

Industry snapshot: coaching wanted

Leaders have a desire to be coached. In 2013, Stanford University and the Miles Group polled over 200 chief executive officers (CEOs), board direc-tors, and senior executives of North American private and public enter-prises. Those at the CEO level who responded held positive opinions toward coaching. Moreover, almost all stated that they enjoyed the process of be-ing coached and receiving leadership advice. However, two-thirds of them were not currently receiving outside assistance. What is more, nearly half of the senior executives had no current outside coaching or leadership input.

Of the coaching package, those at the CEO and director levels pointed toward team building skills as the crucial leadership skills they were currently developing. They also considered these as being most relevant for their own personal development (Larcker *et al.*, 2013).

Individual coaching demonstrates tangible results. Research done by the Association for Talent Development (ATD), for example, found that coaching enhances communication (69 percent), raises engagement (65 percent), heightens skills-to-performance transfer (63 percent), and boosts productivity (61 percent) (ATD, 2014). Research carried out by the Chartered Institute of Personnel and Development (CIPD) echoes these results. In its 2015 annual report, the Institute noted that coaching has become an increasingly common intervention for supporting effective development, with coaching identified by 40 percent of the respondents with talent management activities as one of the three most used development practices indeed. To add to this, 45 percent of the respondents thought this was one of the three most effective activities. Furthermore, almost two-thirds of surveyed respondents stated that the use of coaching by peers or line managers would increase within their enterprises over the next two years (CIPD, 2015).

According to the 2016 Global Coaching Study, undertaken by the International Coach Federation (ICF), the coaching profession is growing as a result. Building upon an impressive sample of 15,380 respondents from 137 countries, the Federation believes that there are 53,300 professional coaches worldwide, generating around US\$2.356 billion in annual revenue. In this 2016 review, the Federation also collected information about individuals who label themselves as managers and team leaders who apply coaching skills. Of those reporting that they deploy coaching skills, 54 percent self-identified as managers and team leaders within their enterprises. In addition, more than half of the managers and team leaders who use coaching (57 percent) see it as a skill-set (ICF, 2016).

And, finally, coaching should be integrated with change leadership efforts to build positive change capabilities and change teams, increase change friendliness and readiness, overcome resistance, promote resilience, develop change agents, and lead an agile culture. In point of fact, in 2018, the Human Capital Institute (HCI) and the International Coach Federation (ICF) partnered to research change management and the role of coaching in change management efforts. Their study, "Building a Coaching Culture for Change Management," based on 432 completed questionnaires and interviews with subject-matter experts, finds that coaching-related activities are rated the most helpful in achieving the goals of change management initiatives. For example, 67 percent reported that team coaching with a professional coach practitioner helped achieve the goals of the change management initiative, as opposed to, say, web-based training or e-learning, which was reported as very and extremely helpful by 34 percent only. Besides, their research demonstrates that among organizations with a strong coaching culture, 61 percent are also classified as high-performing organizations.

Among enterprises without a strong coaching culture, just 27 percent are also regarded as high-performing organizations. In other words, strong coaching cultures are more than twice as likely to be high-performing organizations. Further, a strong coaching culture (think: enterprises with a systemic approach to coaching) is correlated with most of the indicators of a high-performing enterprise, including success in customer satisfaction, shareholder value, profitability, labor productivity, and large-scale strategic change. Ultimately, using coaching to develop leaders to lead an agile culture is correlated with respondents' greater confidence in employees' abilities to plan for change ($r = .17$, $p <.01$) and execute change ($r = .18$, $p <.05$) (HCI/ICF, 2018).

Developing high-quality teams

Leaders seldom work alone. Recently, the nature of work has become incredibly complex; individual leaders will not triumph on their own. For that reason, great teamwork and work teams are essential to the success of any senior leader and thriving organization. Nonetheless, teams do not develop overnight. Rather, they evolve, and the team's leadership may change in time.

Latest research has concentrated on expert, innovative work teams. For example, studying 735 French companies, research finds that board selection and appointment can be a strategic change for innovation, that is to say, companies with high innovation intensity hire directors with distinct skills, and different forms of innovation really need different profiles of directors in terms of board capital – human (education and experience) and social capital (relationships and networks). Specifically, organizations with a high innovation intensity would select directors with a PhD degree, as holding a doctorate reflects experience in research. Besides, firms with a high innovation intensity would appoint directors with marketing and communication expertise, whereas financial expertise is not required (favorable outcomes of innovation activities are conditional on their successful operational execution, which calls for design and creativity) (Allemand *et al.*, 2017; Zenou *et al.*, 2020). Further, a Harvard Business School/Hay Group research project that examined senior teams around the globe revealed that effective teams can significantly contribute to their enterprises, yet only one in five are extremely good, while one-third are mediocre, and 42 percent are poor. The study identified "a clearly defined senior leadership team" as one of the conditions for effective operations – rather than a single heroic CEO (Wageman *et al.*, 2008).

The best way to support organizational success is to build teams to achieve ambitious goals, collectively. Clearly, individual executive coaching is an established method of development, and much has been published on individual skill acquisition. Yet, executive leadership team (ELT) coaching is far less common and not much has been published on the methods or success of coaching task-performing ELTs.

The greater complexity of numbers or the collection of individual team members is not what team-focused coaching for change leadership and engagement is about. In a team setting, the client is the entirety of the relationship system itself. The interdependent performance, behavior, and relational energy of a team-focused coaching session are greater than just the sum of its individual members. Team establishment is not a social event only, rather, ELTs are to be developed to perform work effectively, not just mix well. Time is required for a productive team to gel, and even more time and energy are needed for a senior leadership team to meld and reach peak performance and effectiveness. Team coaching aids the team in the performance of their designated tasks and in achieving tangible goals. Of greater importance, coaching enables teams to generate the synergy that fuels even higher performance effectiveness.

In developing a coordinated and task-oriented team, a dynamic process is undertaken. The model that was first introduced by Tuckman in 1965 and revisited in 1977 (Tuckman & Jensen, 1977), provides a description of the five stages of small-group development that is typical in building high-powered teams. In the *forming* stage, the team will set out its mandate, priorities, tasks, and intentions. Next, the team will frame strategic choices; in this *storming* phase, differences become apparent. In the subsequent *norming* phase, individual team members embrace other members' positions, and the team constructively devises outputs. Functioning teams will then move on to *performing*. This is the stage where the team is fully present and high performing. In the final phase, *adjourning*, the task-performing team's program closes and the team learns from the engagement and carries the experience into their future endeavors.

Having said that, in practice, teamwork – especially innovative teamwork – is not so unambiguous. Rather, it can be a lot more confusing, and progress is hardly ever made through such elegant and linear processes (Super, 2020). Therefore, a competent executive team coach will *dynamically* mix different coaching approaches. These include the motivational, strategy-related, consultative, and educational aspects of coaching. The intent is to respond to the team's life cycle and development stage. Hackman and Wageman (2005) put forward a rigorous theory of team coaching, and hold the opinion that team coaching can boost team effectiveness only when four conditions are in place:

1. The processes critical to team performance effectiveness (e.g., collective effort, creative collaboration, team member knowledge and skills, and task-appropriate performance strategy) are without constraint by task or corporate demands.
2. The team is structured well and the business entity champions it, rather than placing obstacles to the team's work.
3. Coaching is focused upon salient task performance processes and not on the members' interpersonal links or on activities that are outwith the team's mandate.
4. Team coaching is deployed only when the team is ready for it.

Clearing the air: team-centered coaching for positive change and engagement

Change involves the expenditure of energy, and continuing the process of leading sustainable change involves sustaining positive energy. For teams to be brilliantly effective, they need to have a positive working climate where the team members can work – and work with pleasure. Enjoying being around the people is one indication of your team being effective (Parker, 2006). Teams tend to thrive in a positive team climate, namely, organizational contexts that are supportive of collaborative functioning groups. There are four aspects crucial to a positive team climate: (1) offering participative and psychological safety of team members making decisions and having everyone's view being listened to; (2) supporting innovation; (3) having a clear vision; and (4) being task-focused – with the team committed to achieving the highest possible standards of task performance (Anderson & West, 1996).

Although positive strategic transformation is needed more than gold or oil, and the ability to lead positive change is an essential skill these days, no matter what title and company are on your business card, bringing about successful transformations is not simple. Many large-scale change management programs occur in parallel, adding to the complexity of an already challenging process. In actuality, failure is alarmingly high. Indeed, around 70 percent of organizational change programs fail – irrespective of whether they are driven by "mergers," "acquisitions," "downsizing," "de-layering," "IT," "total quality management," "business process re-engineering," or "culture change" initiatives (Hamlin, 2016).

Negativity and aversion come about in the workplace when transformation shoves and prods people beyond their comfort zones. This shatters team dynamics and cooperation, and such toxic side effects can manifest in a variety of ways. A list of the far too many symptoms includes stress, denial, resistance to change, being critical, attitude trough, distrust, feigning ignorance, perceived breach of psychological contract, fear of failure, procrastination, pursuit of personal agendas, change fatigue, negative relational energy, malicious compliance, agreeing verbally but not following through, and sabotage. Negativity and interference are like old meat and moldy cheese – toxins that drain enthusiasm and energy – and poison a team.

Team coaches must counter this interference, and make team members aware that such behaviors are not in tune with effective teamwork. Team-based coaching can be a powerful antitoxin – an organic, radical way to energize and lead positive change methodologically and creatively. Team-based coaching can bring to the fore alternatives and choices from which the best solutions can be picked out and allowed to flourish in a non-directive, non-judgmental, and almost evangelical manner.

Window on practice: getting from dilemma to solution

Teams need expert coaching (Hackman, 2009). A professional executive coach can do much to energize and facilitate the co-creative process of change, and to aid a senior leadership team to quickly make the leap to the high-performing stage. One such situation I expedited comes to mind. A talent management team under the Chief Human Resource Officer (CHRO) had been tussling with a strategic recruitment issue for three days without a cogent solution. The company, an integrated oil company (IOC), was going international and needed to select a core group to establish and to manage their new overseas plant. The team had considered and discussed several scenarios. Among these were filling key positions with in-house nationals from the parent country, hiring talented individuals who were nationals of the host country, selecting the management team from a region of the world that had strong similarities to the host country, or recruiting effective senior leaders from a Third World country – extremely talented oil and gas (O&G) professionals seeking a breakout opportunity and happy to relocate.

As a team coach, I aided the selectors in recognizing what the team needed. As a result, the team puzzled their way out of the dilemma in but one day. Therein, the team vigorously and strategically wrestled with the problem. We defined the challenge, reframed the strategic choices, threw a few options on the table and clustered them, specified what was needed to make each strategy work, identified the barriers to making the choice, and designed a valid means of testing and removing the key barriers. In the end, the team proposed a game-changing functional formula for the organization not only to establish this plant, but also to set the grounds for it to flourish and dominate in the marketplace.

Getting from dilemma to solution was strategic. Among others, it involved imaginative responses within a team coaching methodology built on three principles: (1) *team* agreement; (2) a *cycle* of energizing, redesigning, and gelling; and (3) a *dialogic* approach to learning. The trio helped develop collaborative behaviors.

Team charter

To enhance the communication of aspirations that lead to success, and to better select the guiding principles and ground rules that a team should adhere to throughout the change coaching journey, a team charter must be designed before any team coaching begins. The creation of such a charter can be a powerful introduction to team coaching, but of fundamental importance, the charter can be crucial if the team goes off-track or becomes dysfunctional.

By means of research, it has been recognized that the derailment of leadership is most likely brought about because of problems with interpersonal relationships, an inability to build and lead a team, an inability to develop or adapt, or failure to meet business objectives (Van Velsor & Leslie, 1995). If the leader normally adds value to the enterprise, and demonstrates a readiness to learn and develop, the enterprise might go all out to help the leader retool and change dysfunctional rituals. Methods that are well established for resetting maladjustment, or for professional development include daily self-coaching "check-ins" (Tkaczyk, 2014), and specialized programs such as "individual coaching for effectiveness" (Hellervik *et al.*, 1992), embracing both diagnosis and customized developmental interventions. A team charter is insurance that any development supports the team's direction, needs, and goals.

The talent management team wrestling with the strategic recruitment issue crafted the following team charter (Box 2.1).

A cycle of energizing, redesigning, and gelling

To assist the action-oriented, work-centric, people operations team to reach an optimal solution and advance performance to the next level, I used a series of stimulating questions that went beyond conventional problem-solving by building on what was working well. That being the case, to establish a

---

Box 2.1 The team charter

- *Winning aspiration*: The team set their goal to be the go-to professionals for any issues related to strategic people operations and for the L&D that executives and winning recruits might need at any time.
- *Team values*: The team considered among their assets, best-in-class capabilities, practical rigor, non-stop learning, high-quality business partnering, creative collaboration, being arrogance-free and entrepreneurially spirited, and viewing change as "managed learning."
- *Team roles and responsibilities*: The strengths of team members were identified and roles were assigned. Some of these were: organizational designer, monitor, resource investigator, futurist, challenger, disturbance handler, and positive energizer.
- *Ground rules*: An agreed code of ethics served as the foundation for any team activity. The ground rules included a commitment to confidentiality, dialogic reflection, openness and appreciative inquiry; keeping the timing and frequency of meetings, and not to cancel a team coaching session unless it was an emergency. Furthermore, agreement was put in place to provide negative feedback positively and developmentally, and to tell the truth without blame or judgment.

---

threefold space of positive energy, collective design thinking, and ambidexterity, I reached for the following team-centered coaching questions from the ERG playbook for positive organizational change and engagement:

Energize

* What energizes your team and gives it life?
* What is already working well – at first glance … at second glance? What "superpowers" do your team members already possess?
* Without being humble, share a story about when your team performed at its peak and completed a task that had a particularly positive impact and made you feel proud to be in such a team. What were the circumstances during that time? Why were you proud? What made that possible?

Redesign

* What is the "Everest goal"/"moonshot" that your team wants to pursue and achieve in a short time … in the distant future?
* Describe the future you want for your team. What does winning mean for you? Use words, expressions, or images that capture your desired future, task outcomes, goals, and objectives.
* If you could not fail, what would be your strategic choices, and which of those choices would add the most value? What would have to be true?

Gel

* Of all the choices you have pondered, which ones do you think you will pursue?
* What action steps will you take right now (today/tomorrow/next week/next month) to accomplish your goal? What milestones, measures, and metrics can you put in place to put the pedal of progress to the floor and power shift toward your goal?
* Who exactly is going to do what exactly and by when exactly? How will you keep on strategizing to win?

Dialogic learning

Dialogue can help a team willingly, genuinely, non-judgmentally, and without interference advance their learning and understanding through free exchange of ideas and intellectual interventions. To facilitate this type of open dialogue, five strategies of inquiry can fundamentally shape and transform the team dynamics:

* Advocate for outcomes by means of suggestions and open inquiry, e.g., "Here's a possibility…," or "What might be appropriate/inappropriate here?"

- Obtain genuine buy-in by asking the team members, "What should we do?" and "How can each of us explain this to colleagues?"
- Clarify by paraphrasing, e.g., "It seems to me that this is what you mean ... To what extent does that capture your point?"
- Resolve differences by asking for more information, e.g., "It seems that you think this argument is not a super idea. I'm not exactly sure how you understand it. Could you help me understand how you see the situation?"
- Deepen understanding by uncovering causes and justifications, e.g., instead of asking "What do you want?" ask, "Why do you want that?" or "Why is that important to you?"

Ultimately, as the requirements for change never end, and as life is always in a state of flux, a team never remains in one space. After the process has "gelled," the whole positive inquiry cycle starts again in iteration to the previous in the face of new tasks or changes or challenges. As the team cycles again through the three stages of energizing, redesigning, and gelling, the, by now, high-quality links between team members are confirmed, sustained, and strengthened. When collective leadership team coaching is working, team members enthusiastically engage in this continuous process and are unwilling to stop and exit the team when the coaching intervention ends.

Next-practice insights

Coaching task-performing executive leadership teams (ELTs) is different from coaching individuals. The study of team-centered coaching for change leadership is an emergent field – it is a work in progress. In today's business world, the majority of enterprises do not currently have robust cultures of team coaching in place, hence, much still needs to be discovered. Advancing the healthy practice of team coaching requires work and advertisement.

Here are some helpful insights into team-centered coaching.

Coaching ELTs for change leadership is *not* optional; like taking in oxygen, it is essential. On being skillfully coached, boards, C-suite, and senior business executive teams will bring about positive change, strategic agility and organizational renewal, heightened organizational learning, better business and personal health, collective creativity for breakthrough results, effectiveness, and performance that are far above the norm.

The team coach's primary responsibility is not to tell the team what to do (telling is *not* coaching), but to minimize interference upon the team so as to help it achieve flow. Talent minus interference is equal to performance. As disturbances are quelled, the potential is increased for team members to actively shape and co-create desired futures. Intended outcomes are achievable when co-active team coaching energizes and equips ELTs with the tools to develop within them, giving them the capabilities necessary for notching up another win.

Evaluation has always been the Achilles' heel of executive L&D, in team coaching, the evaluation gap is clear. In team coaching, the dynamic processes unfold in real time, often in uncertain, task-rich and task-changing environments. A critical approach to the evidence-base nature of team coaching will not only help to close the evaluation gap, it will help to establish credibility. Rigorous evaluation involves measurement by means of both quantitative and qualitative data. Among the possible ways of doing this are measuring team members' reaction and satisfaction via a survey and asking pertinent questions; ascertaining the success of the transfer of team coaching and learning results; recognizing team productivity by both qualitative and quantitative means; recognizing task performance improvements and outputs; measuring team engagement and growth; assessing cultural and behavioral change; establishing mission impact; and assessing quantitatively actual business results, return on expectations (ROE), and calculated return on investment (ROI). Ultimately, the success of individual change leaders as coaches, must be measured too, for instance, by using a 360-degree feedback from key stakeholders on the leaders' performance and behaviors.

The team coaching culture needs to be nurtured. A compelling business case for team coaching as a strategic asset and business partner will help to secure the needed resources, sponsorship, and ownership for team coaching – the time and commitment as well. Team coaching must (and must be seen to) strategically align with business priorities and business metrics such as key performance indicators and organizational targets. Because the need for change is always there, and change efforts necessitate shifts in team functioning, team coaching must be explicitly integrated with change leadership. Furthermore, sufficient evaluation funds must be allocated (and rationally too) so that higher-level evaluation efforts such as return on investment can be evidenced.

Healthy team coaching also implies that ELT coaching is not confused with team training, consulting, mentoring, counseling or therapy. "Cowboys" should *not* be hired. Talent development (TD) professionals must be aware of the mix of coaching delivery methods (motivational, strategic, and knowledge- and skill-acquisition team coaching approaches). In hiring a team coach or developing coaching abilities, the investor should put their money and time in researching and applying effective methodologies to help teams pursue positive, open inquiry-based, collaborative ways of working together.

Ultimately, team coaching is truly an act of *positive collective* leadership. Team coaching skills that emphasize team development and performance effectiveness should be highlighted in the TD portfolios of enterprises. It must be remembered that ongoing senior management team coaching opportunities should be created. When all is said and done, no matter how extremely talented and successful an enterprise's fully-fledged ELT is, there is the need to *always* aim higher.

Summary propositions

Recap and revise the key takeaways from the chapter:

- The study of *team*-centered coaching for change leadership, grounded in *dialogic* Organization Development (OD) and *behavioral* science, is an emergent field. In reality, most enterprises do not currently have robust cultures of team-based coaching in place, and therefore much is still to be learned.

- *Dialogic* OD makes use of *generative conversations* around change issues to help senior leadership teams lead positive strategic organizational change and deliver a creative future.

- Change strategizing treated as a social act, ERG is a *social technology* that enables more stimulating team change conversations and organizational flourishing – in particular, through the power of cultivating creative collaboration, collective reflection, and collective dialogue.

- *Team-focused* coaching does differ from *one-on-one* coaching. Team coaching is not a simple matter of coaching a collection of individuals, but a sophisticated process of coaching a system of interdependent individuals that must build synergistically to achieve a shared outcome. When done well, it can fuel a team's performance for maximum effectiveness.

- A competent executive team coach will dynamically *mix coaching approaches*, such as motivational, strategy-related, consultative, and educational coaching, to respond to the team's lifecycle and development stage.

- The stages of team development are often as follows: *forming, storming, norming, performing*, and *adjourning* (especially relevant to project teams).

- Team coaching can boost team effectiveness only when four *conditions* are in place: (1) corporate or task demands do not constrain the team performance processes that are key to performance effectiveness; (2) the team is well structured and the business champions, rather than interferes with, team work; (3) coaching focuses on salient task performance processes and not on members' interpersonal links or activities that are outwith the team's control; and (4) team coaching is delivered only when the team is ready for it.

- A *positive team climate* is the condition within an enterprise that is supportive of collaboratively functioning work groups.

- Getting from dilemma to solution calls for creative responses within a team coaching methodology built on three principles: (1) *team* agreement; (2) a *cycle* of energizing, redesigning, and gelling; and (3) a *dialogic* approach to learning.

- Team coaching for change leadership and engagement is not a substitute for individual coaching. Rather, it is a complementary process. In a world that is increasingly aware of the power of teams inside and outside organizations, team coaching should be highlighted in the *learning and development portfolios* of organizations in order to nurture senior team development and organizational effectiveness and health.
- Rather than a *best*-practice method, team coaching is a powerful *next*-practice tool for dramatic change and an experience of shared discovery. It helps the enterprise and its employees to go from where they are to where they want or need to be.
- Encouraging effective teamwork is all-important. As Ed Catmull, a cofounder of Pixar and the president of Pixar and Disney Animation Studios, put it: "If you give a good idea to a mediocre team, they will screw it up; if you give a mediocre idea to a great team, they will either fix it or throw it away and come up with something that works" (2008: 68).

Acknowledgments

This chapter is based on "Coaching By Numbers," by B. Tkaczyk in *Ivey Business Journal*, 12/21/2016. Copyright © 2016 Richard Ivey School of Business Foundation (the Richard Ivey School of Business of the University of Western Ontario). The author is grateful to the publisher of the journal for allowing the author to use the published contribution in the book. Also, the author thanks Dawn Oosterhoff and Thomas Watson for their helpful comments on an earlier version.

References for further reading

Allemand, I., Brullebaut, B., Galia, F., & Zenou, E. (2017). Which board members when you innovate? Board selection as a strategic change for innovation. *Strategic Change*, 26(4), 311–322.

Anderson, N., & West, M. (1996). The team climate inventory: Development of the TCI and its applications in teambuilding for innovativeness. *European Journal of Work and Organizational Psychology*, 5(1), 53–66.

ATD. (2014). *The coaching approach: A key tool for successful managers*. Alexandria, VA: The Association for Talent Development.

Catmull, E. (2008). How Pixar fosters collective creativity. *Harvard Business Review*, 86(9), 64–72.

CIPD. (2015). *Learning and development 2015: Annual survey report*. London, UK: The Chartered Institute of Personnel and Development.

Goldsmith, M. (2003). Helping successful people get even better. *Business Strategy Review*, 14(1), 9–16.

Hackman, R. (2009). Why teams don't work: The HBR interview by Diane Coutu. *Harvard Business Review*, 87(5), 98–105.

Hackman, R., & Wageman, R. (2005). A theory of team coaching. *Academy of Management Review*, 30(2), 269–287.

Hamlin, B. (2016). HRD and organizational change: Evidence-based practice. *International Journal of HRD Practice, Policy and Research*, 1(1), 7–20.

Hellervik, L., Hazucha, J. F, & Schneider, R. (1992). Behavior change: Models, methods, and a review of evidence. In M. D. Dunnette & L. M. Hough (Eds.), *Handbook of industrial and organizational psychology* (pp. 823–895). Palo Alto, CA: Consulting Psychologists Press.

HCI/ICF. (2018). *Building a coaching culture for change management*. Cincinnati, OH: Human Capital Institute & Lexington, KY: International Coach Federation.

ICF. (2016). *2016 ICF global coaching study*. Lexington, KY: International Coach Federation.

Larcker, D., Miles, S., Tayan, B., & Gutman, M. (2013). *2013 executive coaching survey*. Stanford, CA: Miles Group and Stanford University.

Parker, G. M. (2006). What makes a team effective or ineffective. In J. V. Gallos (Ed.), *Organization development* (pp. 656–680). San Francisco, CA: Wiley & Sons.

Super, F. (2020). Building innovative teams: Leadership strategies across the various stages of team development. *Business Horizons*, 63(4), 553–563.

Tkaczyk, B. (2014). Daily check-ins stimulate self-improvement. *Talent Development*, 68(8), 72–73.

Tkaczyk, B. (2015). Leading as constant learning and development: The knowledge-creative enterprise. *Design Management Review*, 26(3), 38–43.

Tuckman, B. (1965). Developmental sequence in small groups. *Psychological Bulletin*, 63(6), 384–399.

Tuckman, B., & Jensen, M. A. (1977). Stages of small-group development revisited. *Group & Organization Management*, 2(4), 419–427.

Van Velsor, E., & Leslie, J. B. (1995). Why executives derail: Perspectives across time and cultures. *Academy of Management Perspectives*, 9(4), 62–72.

Wageman, R., Nunes, D., Burruss, J., & Hackman, R. (2008). *Senior leadership teams: What it takes to make them great*. Boston, MA: Harvard Business Press.

Zenou, E., Allemand, I., & Brullebaut, B., & Galia, F. (2020). Board recruitment as a strategic answer: Do companies' strategies for innovation influence the selection of new board members? *Strategic Change*, 29(1), 127–139.

3 ERG strategizing

A professional approach to *positive* human resource and organization development consulting

---

Lead-in

This chapter builds a case for a balanced approach to professional transition consulting, that is, modern consulting based on both relevant strategic transformation practice and highly meticulous business research methods – the "practical rigor." To illustrate this diagnosis-driven organization development (OD) orientation, as an advisory industry snapshot, the chapter benefits from a mini-case study window on practice that foregrounds and relates the key dimensions of the discussion to a real-life business situation. The case study captures how positive organization change was led in a methodological and creative way, by means of the co-creative "energize, redesign, and gel" method, within a training department of a Middle Eastern positioned insurance company – with the aid of a strategic human resource development (HRD) consultancy. Specifically, the positive transformation account records one dramatic organizational development and change effort, i.e., going from a *stiff* "training" function, to one that is *knowledge-creative* "learning and development" (L&D), and strategically aligning the new L&D with business – to effectively execute the organization's design-inspired strategy. The challenge, the method, and the outcome are detailed. In point of fact, this has a direct bearing on HRD/OD consultants (both internal and external), as well as scholars. In reality, if consultants are to "co-create" long-term value and equip their clients with reliable intelligence, then they must be well grounded in knowing and applying scientific research techniques and methods for business. Likewise, scholars must be really plugged into professional relevant practice. It is only through intensely connecting research to performance that we can begin to establish a positive and professional foundation upon which additional strategic discovery- and results-driven HRD/OD consulting work can be built.

Dialogic reflection for professional team development

In your team, discuss the following questions:

1. Why do enterprises have to have reliable intel and insights about their operations?
2. Do you know any diagnostic instruments that can be applied to leading and executing organizational change that you find most helpful or interesting?
3. Does your enterprise have a robust culture of diagnosis-driven organization development in place?
4. What is management consultancy? Why is research essential in consultancy?
5. What is the difference between a generalist consultancy, a boutique firm, and a one-person operation? Does the size of a consulting firm bring different advantages and disadvantages?
6. Who exactly is the client in the client-consultant relationship? What are the success factors in a harmonious client-consultant relationship?
7. What are the habits and qualities of highly professional and effective consultants that must be continuously developed?
8. Are the skills that internal and external consultants apply similar? Do internal consultants have greater problems with credibility than external consultants?
9. "Consultants are always a waste of time." "A consultant is someone who borrows your watch to tell you the time, and then keeps it." "Advice from management consultants is used to support or supersede unpopular business decisions." "We *just* need another new reorg, and we'll be fine!" Do you agree or disagree with these claims? Critically evaluate them.
10. Will, by 2050, the management consultancy industry be very different to what it is today?

> *Helping is a complex phenomenon. The main criterion continues to be that the consultant must be facilitative and helpful.*
>
> (Edgar H. Schein, Sloan Fellows Professor of
> Management Emeritus, MIT Sloan School of Management)

In Chapter 2, we revealed the foundations upon which the *dialogic* organization development (OD) approach toward change leadership is built. In this chapter, to enable its full flowering, we exemplify how a thorough, systematic *diagnostic* OD allied with an effective dialogic OD can create a powerhouse change process. Not using any model is not a real option – whether explicit models (such as the energize, redesign, and gel model) or implicit ones (derived from gained experience – often the limited experience of one or just a few leaders) are adopted, diagnosis *will* exist. Besides, models offer highly practical value. They provide a shared language, make the complexity of a problem manageable by reducing it to a number of workable steps, help determine which organizational activities or components need most attention (and alignment), and spotlight the interconnectedness of organizational variables, such as strategy, design, HR practices, processes, and systems. On that account, this synergistic diagnostic-dialogic extension of the OD approach to change can be recognizably successful in our VUCA (volatile, uncertain, complex, and ambiguous) world of constant change; it positions *positive* OD that is matchless in impacting how change in enterprises is facilitated. As a case in point, let's consider the global consulting industry first, and then one strategic human resource development (HRD) initiative that was effectively led, in the Middle East, by employing the energize, redesign, and gel (ERG) method.

Industry snapshot: the global consulting market

Consulting, one of the world's newest professions, exploded onto the business scene in the United States in the 1930s, in Western Europe in the 1950s, and in Central and Eastern Europe in the 1990s. In the twenty-first century, demand is absolutely booming in the Asia-Pacific region (Gross & Poor, 2008). ALM Intelligence, a US-based analyst firm, estimates the global management consulting market to be worth about $240 billion, while the European Federation of Management Consultancies Associations (FEACO) estimates the market value at nearly $280 billion. Source Global Research, a UK-based analyst firm, provides a more conservative estimate at $120 billion (Acquisdata, 2019).

The United States of America

In the United States, the federal government deems management consultants to be "management analysts." The median annual pay for management analysts was $83,610 in May 2018 (the lowest-paid 10 percent earned less than $48,360, and the highest-paid 10 percent earned more than $152,760). Employment of these professionals is projected to grow 14 percent – from 876,300 in 2018, to 994,600 in 2028. This rate is much faster than the average for all occupations (the average growth rate for all occupations is 5 percent). Growth will be especially enhanced in boutique firms that work exclusively in specific industries or specialize in particular types of business function, such as human resources (BLS, 2019). On top, the US consulting market performed well in 2018, with growth of 8.5 percent, outpacing even 2017's impressive uptick, taking the market to a value of $68.5 billion. Indeed, the healthy economy, stimulated by 2017's tax cut, made for positive market conditions, with client firms in a confident mood and eager to invest; the complexity and pace of change facing clients being the main drivers of demand (Source Global Research, 2019a).

Canada

In Canada, management consulting remains vibrant, adaptable, and vital to the local and global marketplaces. In 2017, the management, scientific and technical services consulting sector achieved operating revenues and operating expenses of $21.3 billion and $15.3 billion, respectively. Most sales were made to domestic businesses (67.8 percent), followed by sales to governments, not-for-profit organizations, and public institutions (13.3 percent), and sales to international clients (13.3 percent). Referring to a breakdown of the management consulting services provided that year, strategic management consulting services represented 20.8 percent of consulting sales, and human resource management consulting services accounted for 12 percent of consulting sales (Statistics Canada, 2019). Interestingly, nowadays, client firms tend to hire consultants to implement their strategies and to educate and train staff. Instead of being generalists, consultants are developing niche proficiencies and more dynamic capabilities, and they are adopting a lot nimbler and more collaborative approach (CMC-Canada, 2016).

The United Kingdom

In the United Kingdom, the statistics published by the Management Consultancies Association (MCA), which takes into its fold 60 percent of the UK management consulting sector (valued at more than £5.5 billion), reveal that the consulting industry enjoyed solid growth in fee income of 8.05 percent in 2015. Although this is down from 8.4 percent in 2014, it remains well ahead of gross domestic product growth and the performance of many other industries. In the field, graduate and other new recruitment continued to be high, with this slice of the industry now taking up more than 45,000 people (up by 9.5 percent compared to 2014). Data on aggregate fee income by service line indicates that digital and technology consulting remains the greatest consulting service and continues in aggrandizement proportionally to the development of the industry: It now represents 27.7 percent of the total spending across the disparate strata. In contrast, strategy consulting represents 9.6 percent of the total expenditure throughout this vast field, while human capital advisory, change management advisory, and business transformation consulting represent 5.7 percent, 5.3 percent, and 4.4 percent, respectively, of the total money endowed across different slices of business consultancy (Management Consultancies Association, 2016). Further, based on 1,806 survey responses from executives, directors, and senior managers in the UK in November and December 2017, and on qualitative research from interviews carried out in 2017 and 2018 with senior buyers of consulting in the UK, the attributes of a firm that clients say are most important to them appear to be changing. Generally, the attribute that clients are most likely to rate as important is an innovative approach – the same one judged last year. Yet, when we reflect upon what's changed since last year, one can observe that price, culture, and ability to execute have become progressively more important to client firms.

On the flip side, quality of thought leadership, brand and reputation, and account management process are among the attributes regarded as slightly less significant now than they were last year. Perhaps a shift in clients' concern, from planning their transformation agenda to action, could partly be the explanation (Source Global Research, 2018a). Although 2019 was a difficult year for the UK consulting industry, because of the uncertainty caused by Brexit, the year 2019 did deliver 4.1 percent growth in the consulting market, with 2020's performance not expected to be significantly different. In particular, 2019 was an unfortunate period for financial services. All the same, clients have been eager for digital transformation services (DX) (such as the cloud, data analytics, and cybersecurity), and for sustainability work (including clients, for example, in the energy sector), which is a fundamental change of direction for numerous consultancies that earlier were fiercely focused on partner revenue streams (Source Global Research, 2020a).

Central and Eastern Europe, excluding the Russian Federation

With reference to Central and Eastern Europe (CEE), excluding Russia, 2017 saw a solid year of growth for the consulting market, with each and every market in the region growing faster than in 2016. Although lagging behind Western Europe, digital transformation was the main driver of consulting demand, with robotic process automation work playing a pivotal role in this. After holding at about 5 percent growth for the past several years, CEE's consulting market (excluding Russia) saw more significant growth of 6.7 percent in 2017, with Poland, an EU country, upgraded to "developed market" status in indices run by FTSE Russell. Moreover, Poland, the region's largest market, once again saw the highest growth rate, followed by Slovakia and the Czech Republic (Source Global Research, 2018b).

Eastern Europe and the Russian Federation

Now the entire Eastern Europe *and* Russia market is estimated to be worth €2,949 million (Source Global Research, 2019b). Be that as it may, for advisors in Russia, the past few years were difficult – with international sanctions, a collapse in oil prices, and a drop in the value of the ruble all negatively affecting clients' readiness to launch extra projects. Although 2017 saw some greater interest in digital transformation work in Russia, not all consultancies grew in 2017 (especially consulting on people operations, human resource management (HRM) outsourcing, HR policy execution, but also investment advice, and risk management), and HR and change management consultancies had another tough year (decline rate 2017: -1.1 percent) (Source Global Research, 2018c).

The Asia-Pacific region

While consulting in Europe continues to grow, the outlook is distinctly positive for growth of the consultancy business in the Asia-Pacific region. The Asia-Pacific management consulting industry was forecast to break through the $50 billion barrier in 2018 (Consultancy.Asia, 2018). Specifically, the four most attractive locations are Australia, Japan, India, and China.

The Commonwealth of Australia

In Australia, consultants interviewed for the 2018 research report indicated that the recipe for the 7.1 percent growth the consulting market experienced in 2017 was largely a simple function of the nation's sound economy. Australia's near-legendary economic performance – in 2017, Australia celebrated 26 consecutive years of GDP growth – has been a major driver in consulting demand for some time now, with optimistic clients keen to make big investments in growth opportunities and transformation programs (Source Global Research, 2018d). The year 2018 was also a golden year for Australia's advisors, with the market growing 8.1 percent (a tangible improvement on 2017's already continued expansion) to reach a total value of US$5,408 million (Source Global Research, 2019c).

Japan

As for Japan, Japan's consulting market experienced significant growth of 9.3 percent in 2018, and most consultancies speak highly of the state of the market, and are rather bullish on the prospects throughout 2020. Largely, this is due to the maturity of Japan's wider economy. On top of that, clients seek to diversify their portfolios (e.g. by investing in start-ups), plus they need help with start-up operations in other countries (Source Global Research, 2019d).

The Republic of India

With reference to India, 2018 was a very good year for consultants in India, with the market continuing to expand by more than 17 percent. While not reaching the heights of the 18.2 percent growth of 2017, advisors were still mostly positive about the market's performance, with 2018's performance well up on the sub-14 percent increases of the mid-2010s (Source Global Research, 2019e).

The People's Republic of China

Regarding China, 2017 was also another good year for advisors being engaged in China. They profited from the nation's strongest economic growth in two years and a progressively mature client base with a deepening appreciation of what management consulting could do. Here, one of the prevailing trends driving strong consulting market performance is an aggressive growth agenda (Source Global Research, 2018e). Yet, while advisors remain fairly positive, some are beginning to lose sleep. Since the start of 2019, the trade war with the US has escalated rapidly, leading to a further slowing of GDP growth – a tendency it is believed will continue at least through 2020 (Source Global Research, 2019f). Ultimately, in a highly fluid situation, depending on the scenario, both China's and the global GDP in 2020 could slide or fall significantly due to the COVID-19 outbreak.

The Middle East

Relating to the Middle East, the Gulf Cooperation Council (GCC) consulting market grew an extraordinary 9.1 percent, cracking the $3 billion mark for the first time in 2018. In particular, the market in Saudi Arabia, representing almost half of all consulting spend across the GCC, saw good levels of growth in 2019, mainly due to the National Transformation Program (NTP). The transition program, launched to diversify the country's economy away from their dependence on oil, generated increased demand for consulting services. Likewise, the United Arab Emirates (UAE), the GCC's second-largest consulting market, performed very strongly, with steady growth and an overall take of ca. $850 million. What's more, organizations in the UAE continued to seek professional advisory services, with demand looking very positive into 2019 (Source Global Research, 2019g). In 2019, the GCC consulting market proceeded vigorously too – overall growth of almost 10 percent in 2019 topped 2018's 9.1 percent uptick, which in turn was better than 2017's performance. A healthy appetite for consulting continues to build up (consulting demand being driven commonly by transformation and transition efforts), with governments across the region putting money into minimizing dependency on oil revenues and so seeking consultancies to help them execute their diversification and transformation plans (Source Global Research, 2020b).

Disadvantages of consultants

Despite this impressive rate of growth, consultants are still viewed with many misgivings. The saw that "A consultant is someone who borrows your watch to tell you the time, and then keeps it" still is posted on websites and given a thumbs-up. Those who undervalue the profession often tend to view consultants as a screen or scapegoat for unpopular strategic decisions, while others avoid them like the plague, precisely because they fear the diagnosis.

Such cynical or critical views, however, are occasionally grounded in reality. External consultants can fail to live up to their hype when they rebadge existing organizational practices, introduce fads, trade in banal management rhetoric, offer cookie-cutter remedies and, like the traveling medicine showman, peddle untested miracle cures, or like a medieval ceremony foment secrecy rather than offer real value. This darker side of the consulting field has been well substantiated by numerous researchers (Berglund & Werr, 2000; Clark, 1995; Clark & Fincham, 2002; Clark & Salaman, 1998a; 1998b; Clegg, Kornberger, & Rhodes, 2004; Collins, 2004; Craig, 2005; Fincham, 2000; Heusinkveld & Benders, 2005; Kantola & Seeck, 2011; Kieser 2002; Kipping & Clark, 2012; Phelan, 2013; Saint-Martin, 2004; Sturdy, Clark, Fincham, & Handley, 2009; Tkaczyk, 2018).

In similar fashion, when an organization's HR professionals take on an internal consultant role, the results may be less than what was intended and often much of a headache. For example, when serving as a "business partner" in a restructuring process, HR staff members may find that their role as "employee advocates" is diminished precisely at a time when some tea and sympathy are needed. Moreover, the boss may be quite irritated when the consultancy team throws their cards on the table and will seek retribution rather than agree to reform. Such reconfigured relationships (which would not even be possible in small businesses with few employees) may also create tensions and challenges within the HR function, and even lead to silos or fragmentation within the HR department that smother any hope of organizational improvement (Caldwell, 2003; 2008; CIPD, 2004; CRF, 2009; Francis & Keegan, 2006; Hope-Hailey, Farndale, & Truss, 2005; Pickard, 2005; Reilly & Williams, 2006).

HRD and OD consulting

Because organizations always had and always will have people and organizational development issues, there will invariably be the need for expert consultants in the field of human resource and organization development (HRD/OD). HRD activity first gained a recognizable organizational identity in the United States in the 1970s. Therein, it was defined as a series of harmonized activities carried out within a specific period of time that are designed to induce behavioral change (Nadler, 1970). By the 1980s, with regard to HRD, movement was made toward a more strategic orientation that encompassed the identification of required skills and the active management of learning to best exploit bona fide effective business strategies for the long-range future (Hall, 1984), as well as consulting (ASTD, 1980). In this respect, HRD consulting was important in maintaining the health and sanity of the enterprise. By the early 1990s, HRD was considered a profession of importance in the business field, wherein the practitioners served as change agents for both individual and organizational renewal (Burack, 1991). Further, it was proposed that integrating HRD research and practice requires that a more suitable approach be taken when scholars and practitioners collaborate with each other (Jacobs, 1997). With reference to OD:

[It is] a process of planned and emerging interventions utilizing behavioral and organizational science principles to change a system and improve its effectiveness, conducted in accordance with values of humanism, participation, choice, and development so that the organization and its members learn and develop.

(Jamieson, 2015: 9)

What is more, OD activities, based on a broad base of behavioral science knowledge, to ensure the best fit between the organizational and individual goals, aim to achieve a pragmatic enhancement of organizational capabilities – improving intra-organizational efficiency and performance, including those capabilities dealing with individual health and psychological well-being at work (King & Anderson, 2002). Today, HRD and OD consultants and practitioners can turn to international organizations such as the Academy of Human Resource Development (AHRD), the Association for Talent Development (ATD; formerly the American Society for Training and Development, or ASTD), the Chartered Institute of Personnel and Development (CIPD), and the Organization Development (OD) Network for continuing professional development and guidance. As of 2020, the AHRD has a membership of more than 500 HRD practitioners active in more than 39 countries (Academy of Human Resource Development, 2020), the ATD is representing more than 30,000 talent development (TD) professionals, operating in more than 120 countries (Association for Talent Development, 2020), the CIPD is the voice of a multinational community of 150,000 HR and learning and development (L&D) professionals around the world (CIPD, 2020), and the OD Network, the largest international association of OD practitioners in the world, established in 1968 by founders in the field of OD, serves change agents by building a global community for exchanging best practices, opportunities to interact with thought leaders and access to leading-edge organization and human systems development practices, tools and technologies (Organization Development Network, 2020).

Human asset accounting and utilization

The notion of people as capital is rooted in economic studies (Becker, 1964; 1993). Herein, economic value is often equated with *capital* – money or property utilized to turn a profit. Employers had, however, unfortunately, routinely considered the HR function (being thought to be for the most part workforce-centered) as a cost rather than as a value generator for their enterprises (Cascio & Boudreau, 2015; Schultz, 1961). This misapprehension resulted in investment in human capital assets being habitually the first to be cut if there was a downturn in the enterprise, its industry or the broader economy. In other words, the workers often got the shaft so that their bosses could keep the mine.

The reality is that, over time; the profession of HR has shifted from a workforce-centered *reactive* personnel management (PM) approach, to a *strategic* resource-focused HR orientation (Guest, 1987). In supplying the firm with a pool of human capital, HR has come to be considered to be crucial for creating and holding competitive advantage and strategic value (Wright, McMahan, & McWilliams, 1994). By determining who provides a service or expertise for an organization for a particular issue, and whether these advisors consult flawlessly, strategic HR and HRD have a key role in the design and maintenance of the business performance metrics of productivity, quality, innovation, employee engagement, customer satisfaction, and profitability.

CIPD research, built upon the opinions of 143 HR leaders and 152 non-HR leaders, has noted that a majority of leading people in business agree on both current and future business priorities. Accordingly, cost management was cited as the most common current priority by 63 percent of all HR leaders and 61 percent of all non-HR leaders, and as a future priority by 54 percent and 55 percent, respectively. In addition, both HR leaders and non-HR leaders burn the midnight oil over many of the same issues, for example, managing costs while delivering priorities, and making sure they have the talent and leadership capabilities they require. Of relevance to our argument is that leadership capability heads the HR leaders' challenge list and was the second most common challenge for the non-HR group (41 percent and 27 percent, respectively). Still, even though both sets of leaders are mostly aligned on the top priorities, their views diverge when it comes to establishing HR's contribution to their achievement. In particular, 72 percent of all HR leaders agree that their current HR or people strategy did and will boost the possibilities of their enterprise achieving its future key priorities in three years' time, but only 26 percent of all the non-HR leaders polled thought so (CIPD, 2016).

Relating to strategic HRD and the construction of a culture of learning in particular, an ATD study of 832 TD leaders, of whom nearly two-thirds represented national or multinational enterprises with more than 1,000 employees, indicated that robust and thriving cultures of learning and development are distinct hallmarks of enterprises that continuously achieve excellent business results. Furthermore, top performers are five times more likely to have a learning culture. Yet, the study also found out that only 31 percent of all polled organizations have well-developed learning cultures (Association for Talent Development, 2016a). On top of that, the state of learning and development evaluation had not changed significantly. In addition, while 88 percent of the survey participants affirmed that their enterprises do measure the reactions of employees participating in training sessions, only 35 percent of all the organizations that responded measured the business results of the proffered learning programs, and only 15 percent measured the return on investment (ROI) of such efforts (Association for Talent Development, 2016b). As the following case study illustrates, strategic HRD consultants can play a significant role in transforming a moribund, stale, dull as dishwater, bureaucratic training function into an agile, dynamic, knowledge-centered learning and development unit.

Window on practice: leading positive organizational change

At an insurance company based in the Middle East that serves individuals, families, professionals, SMEs, and corporate and banking clients internationally, a results-driven HRD consultancy effort entered the starting gate by appreciating the three core domains of strategically integrated HRD: (1) organizational learning; (2) organizational performance; and (3) organizational change (Gilley & Gilley, 2003). To innovate, boost flexibility and resourcefulness, grab hold of new opportunities arising from geopolitical volatility, and to leave its competitors in the dust, the company crafted a new business strategy: *enterprise agility*. To achieve this, the company's leaders recognized that they needed an adaptable organizational design that would positively affect their training department. Hence, they sought outside advice on how to transform their bland, centralized, and mechanistic training function into a nimble, learning-ready one.

In October 2015, company management sent letters off to several competing consultancies, asking each to propose an initial solution (including approach, models, tools), fee structure, and work plan with quality control and management measures. At the time, the firm did not have a people management strategy in place that would encompass *strategic* TD. Instead, the head of training merely reported to the company's director of personnel management and planning and simply provided a list of various courses for employees to sign up for. Of the consultancy proposals that were submitted, the insurance company selected one that recommended transforming the training function into a flexible knowledge-creative L&D one. The intent was that this entity would focus on organization-wide learning and development, organizational renewal, and breakthrough innovation (Tkaczyk, 2015a).

At this point, a consulting project manager was brought in to beef up the project team and bring into the fold the necessary mix of associates, consultants, and a case team leader who were in the know about not only strategic HRD and positive OD and change, but also about the insurance industry and the region in which the firm operated. All the project team members were employees of the advisory firm. One month was allotted and kept to for initial assessment and framework design, the actual design of the initiative took another month, the development of design details took a month and a half, and full implementation took an additional three and one-half months, for a total of seven months.

Positive strategic transformation: balancing a strong grounding in scientific research techniques with their creative application

Embedded in the concepts of positive organizational scholarship (Cameron, Dutton, & Quinn, 2003; Cameron & Spreitzer, 2012), design thinking (Austin & Devin, 2003; Boland & Collopy, 2004; Brown, 2009; *CMR*, 2020; *DMI Review*, 2015; Lockwood, 2009; Martin, 2009), and organizational ambidexterity – particularly super-flexibility (Bahrami & Evans, 2010; 2011), the HRD consultants, in pursuing this inspired transformation, proposed to lead the organizational change in a methodological *and* creative manner. The avenue to *positive* transformation that they recommended and that was ultimately selected was to *energize, redesign*, and *gel* (ERG) the change effort and the enterprise. This required a clear strategic framework for thinking about organizational change and development, and agreement on what is to happen, and a route map for executing the various elements of the framework.

In order to endow the client with sufficient reliable intelligence and insights so as to drive decision-making, the consultants deployed both a qualitative (phenomenological) and a quantitative (empirical) approach. To gather the necessary data, the former included participant observation, semi-structured interviews, and delving into existing documentation and reports. The latter utilized surveys and questionnaires, and business process simulations to model operations and enhance the learning function.

A breakdown of each strategic change phase and the related dynamic call to arms follows. Although it is practical to separately address each stage, it must be remembered that they are elements of a dynamic continuous and concurrent process that has become embedded in the insurance firm's day-to-day strategizing routine.

Energize

The following actions were part and parcel of this phase:

- *Performance analysis*: An ERG scorecard was used to appraise such notions as leadership qualities, organizational structures and roles, management practices, employee performance management, employee involvement, customer care, organizational design, and strategic direction. Further, a pre-change audit of system-wide fitness for organizational change and an inquiry into past change initiatives were carried out. Also, internal and external pressures for change were measured.
- *Building a compelling case for change*: To promote enthusiasm for the organizational change and development effort and to connect with employees, positive leadership storytelling sessions and collaborative change conversations took place, both on and off company time and on and off-site. The business narratives centered on five domains: using narrative to ignite action and bring to the fore fresh ideas; transmitting corporate values; getting things done collaboratively; sharing knowledge, and leading the company into the "Promised Land."
- *Strengths-finding*: Assessments were run to identify and profile in-house talents. This action beefed up their newly established continuing professional development (CPD) portfolios. The CPD portfolios comprised two components: a "check-in" and a "design." The check-in is a self-managed disciplined development system. Here, employees *continuously* self-assess by asking *reflective* questions regarding critical and

opportunistic incidents that occurred in the workplace or outside, daily or in the previous week. The design is another self-guided development mechanism. Here, people *continuously* design their own learning by making *developmental* inquiries regarding what they still want to learn and develop, and note how exactly they would execute their development plan – whether infield, outfield, or out of the ballpark.

- *Recruiting "positive change energizers" from within*: Organizational network analysis and advanced statistical mapping were applied to further apprise and measure positive energy networks (the individualistic patterns of energizing relationships and positive connections to others) and to identify positive change energizers (to uncover engaged, proactive, and unselfish individuals who energize the workplace and stimulate progress via self-initiative or teamwork). To do so, a pulse survey was administered via an app to suss out the change effort participants' level of energy, engagement, and job satisfaction.
- *Socializing*: An audit was run of the workplace's positive cultural assets, such as the level and reach of co-determination at both the team and individual levels. Three positive leadership and organizational renewal strategy off-site meetings were also convened to strengthen social bonds among participants and further energize and re-imagine the workplace.

Redesign

This phase took in the following actions:

- *Involving HR and non-HR leaders in collaboration* that is of a strategic nature and in collective design thinking (DT), so as to co-create a blueprint for the new, nimble, dynamic, innovative, pro-active, yeast-raised L&D function, as well as to flesh out its strategy and set down on paper all appropriate performance indicators. This took place as a three-day appreciative inquiry-based, future search summit to engage and convince stakeholders and to encourage the participation of the company's HR leaders and non-HR leaders. It included the chairman and general manager, the director and assistant general manager, 11 board directors, and nine heads of departments.
- *Crafting an agile L&D strategy*: A newly designed "Developing Energized and Talented Workforce for Future Success" strategy embraced experiential learning and job experiences (learning on the job and from project reviews, job enlargement, rotation, and sabbaticals); interpersonal and social learning (coaching, team coaching, mentoring, reverse-mentoring, self-development groups, challenge camps, virtual team learning); assessment (profiling inventories, development assessment centers, 360-degree feedback); self-managed L&D (with daily check-ins); L&D events (including executive education workshops on leading *positive* organizational change); on-demand micro-learning and

real-time cloud-based learning; and gamified learning through serious tailored video games. Developed to boost productivity and engagement, such games were also designed to assess and predict, from the player's performance, their level of curiosity; creativity; competition; rules-bound actions; ability to prioritize, convert tasks into workplace habits, and to learn from mistakes. They were also intended to reveal social intelligence, and, in particular, learning agility. Learning agility, herein, is defined as a strong tendency to display agility in six areas: self-awareness, continuous learning, mental alertness, people skills, self-change, and results orientation.

- *Coaching for positive change leadership and learning aptitude*: Solution-focused, high-performance team and psychological capital coaching interventions were held. Coaching for generative change program participants was done on a one-on-one basis, twice a month, and was undertaken by external coaches hired by the consultancy. Ongoing positive leadership team coaching was also put into practice.
- *Addressing inevitable power struggles and conflicts*: Crafting the new L&D strategy, for example, led one training officer to act in a dysfunctional and arrogant manner. Although feedback regarding his negative routines was delivered positively, it did not help. Specialized individual coaching for effectiveness (ICE) was provided to offer him behavioral alternatives, but that did not bring any positive results, either. To minimize his de-energizing impact on others, the training officer was withdrawn from the change program, but he kept on diminishing others and draining the positive energy and vigor of his colleagues. Eventually, he was dismissed from the company and the company was better for it.
- *Running disciplined experiments*: Before rollout, learning launches were run to minimize risks to the implementation of the change program. Proposed action-outcome hypotheses of record about how the initiative would succeed were put to the test in terms of their value (*Will the client want and pay for it?*), scalability (*Will revenues exceed costs at scale?*), defensibility (*Can we protect advantage?*), and execution (*Can we deliver it flawlessly?*).

Gel

This phase encompassed the following actions:

- *Heat mapping and just-in-time traffic light systems*: Different metrics (including quantitative, qualitative, leading, lagging, financial, and non-cost) were visually tracked on heat maps to continuously monitor and measure performance. In addition, a traffic light data system that brought from the dark the progress of change initiatives in real time helped assure that decisions were based on evidence. In this highly visual tool, notations made in red indicate chaotic performance or a shift in the wrong direction. Such effects are major concerns that are likely to prevent completion of any project. Notations in amber warn that performance is static or not headed toward the desired direction, and minor to moderate concerns about progress are highlighted. Finally, notations in green mean that performance was moving in the desired state, the road is smooth, free of pot-holes, the vista is wide open, the gas tank is full, and there's no traffic ahead – that it was time put on some good driving music and enjoy the ride.

- *Celebrating quick wins*: Relevant wins were publicized on the company's Intranet and screen savers, in email messages, and on bulletin boards at the company's branches in order to generate more short-term wins. What is more, significant wins were celebrated during corporate retreats.
- *Transferring know-how assets and integrating lessons learned*: To bring together accumulated intellectual resources and juice up continuous improvement, new knowledge, ideas, processes, and learning insights were electronically documented and disseminated.
- *Maintaining the momentum*: Continuous reinforcement underlined the conviction that the improvement effort would not gel until all the company's beliefs, behaviors, and assumptions had been fine-tuned and the company was rumbling along like a Harley-Davidson Road King along US Highway 101.
- *Strategizing to win*: The firm's leaders went on to strategize ways to keep self-regenerating through continuous, experiential, social, and reflective learning, through collective design thinking, experimentation, open innovation, and self-organization. This also included various trend-spotting activities. The company was truly rolling and rocking.

The results of the company's efforts

The positive organizational change and development program successfully helped the insurance firm to reconceptualize, redesign, and strategically transform its reactive training function into a nimble knowledge-creative learning and development one. The intended change results were achieved in three ways:

1. Strategic, organizational-wide integration.
2. Alternative evaluation standards.
3. A complete paradigm U-turn.

Strategic, organizational-wide integration

The company's leaders realized the need for an HR strategy encompassing agile and competitive L&D. Thus, HRD became critical. People came to be regarded as the key to competitive advantage. Now an integral and crucial piece of the organization's structure, the agile L&D function, as stated by the company's chairman:

> operates at the strategic level, and is considered a core competence. Actually, the business and L&D are strategically integrated and interdependent. The new L&D adopted a learning approach to strategizing and leading change as "managed learning." This helped us nurture and boost our adaptability and creativity big time. In fact, the program gelled our whole enterprise to the max. Instead of spoon-feeding or jockeying with each other, we now understand each other better and pull in the same direction.

Alternative evaluation standards

Going from minimizing costs to maximizing utilization (human asset accounting and reporting), the new evaluation process gauged six dimensions of the program: (1) ROI (quantifying the financial results of the program, calculated as the net benefit divided by the program costs, multiplied by 100 to convert it to a percent); (2) business impact (actual sales volume rating); (3) intangible results (manifested by the new emphasis on openness to external clients); (4) behavioral changes on the job (as indicated by on-the-job observation and follow-up); (5) learning results (an assessment of learning transfer and intake via, for example, micro-learning and cloud-based quizzes); and (6) participants' reaction and satisfaction (measured via a cloud-based app that worked out staff reaction, energy, engagement, and satisfaction in real time, and applied data-driven, predictive talent, and learning analytics).

In the opinion of the company's CFO:

> Allocating resources to really studying the impact and determining financial results of L&D was super smart. Now L&D is a major business process; it isn't a case of old wine in a new bottle ... We're beginning to capture the ROI, and it's becoming readily apparent. I'm positive that both our internal and external stakeholders and shareholders will appreciate and view human capital assets and L&D metrics as another indicator of value.

The former head of training, who is now the L&D business partner, added:

> It's little wonder that so many change efforts fail. Most of them seem to rest on a slim and unreliable evidence base ... We began to come to the table with evidence and data (and not with ... lunch, ha!). To renew our business and boost our bottom line, we managed to successfully link people, design-led strategy, learning, and sustained performance in a complex world. Learning has become the new currency. Becoming more

evidence-based and analytical empowered us to influence, interact, and enact, rather than just react. Apart from championing value-adding L&D, we promoted unlearning, too. That wasn't all smooth sailing, but workable. We've always hoped to be *by* the table, and not *on* the table ... Now, we feel we finally made it.

A complete paradigm U-turn

The old orientation, represented by a course-based training function, was seen by employees and non-HR leaders as trainer-centered, stiff, centralized, ad-hoc, bureaucratic, compliance-crazy, mechanistic, menu-driven, reactive, and short-term – not to mention something to avoid like the plague. In contrast, the new learning and development function was being identified by employees and company leaders from within and outside HR as learner-centered, agile, energized, holistic, design-centric, humanistic, just-in-time, on-demand, commitment-focused, knowledge-led, organic, integrated, strategic, networked, proactive, fun, and long-term – and like meat to a hungry bear, it was enthusiastically accepted.

The company leaders are now pondering the ways in which they could strategize to win outside their home base (Tkaczyk, 2015b). In particular, they are trying to determine how to sell internal L&D expertise to a key shareholder, a multinational bank. The head of strategy says:

> We're analyzing the commercialization of our new and agile L&D in which we now have a significant level of expertise. We don't want to rest on our laurels; we're future-focused. We can grow, go outside of our country, and be, in fact, a profit center.

The chemistry: essential aspects of a high-quality client-consultant relationship

The first step in a successful consultancy assignment is to identify who is the client. In general terms, the client is the enterprise that employs the services of a consultancy. This contractual relationship is set out in a formal agreement that clearly details arrangements, responsibilities, obligations, and restrictions. Although having such an agreement in place eases the bureaucratic agony of the interaction, too many advisors make the mistake of failing to personalize it.

The human chemistry underlying the client-consultant system is tortuous. As categorized by Schein (1987; 1997), the client representation can be by several distinct individuals, including:

- *Contact clients:* They reach out to the consultant first.
- *Intermediate clients:* They engage in setting up meetings, in organizing, fact-finding, reviewing choices and possibilities, etc.

- *Main clients:* They need the help for which the consultant was hired; they own the problem.
- *Unwitting* or *primary clients:* They will be affected by interventions but are not necessarily aware of this.
- *Indirect clients:* They are aware that they will be affected by the interventions, but are unknown to the consultant.
- *Contract clients:* They work out and sign a contract with the consultant.
- *Ultimate clients:* These include the community, the total enterprise, an occupational group, or any other group that the consultant must deal with. Although they may not work directly with the consultant, their interests and welfare ultimately will be affected by the consulting project.
- *Sponsoring clients:* They provide financial resources for the consultancy and may or may not wish to play a part in establishing the steps that follow or in choosing the consultants.

This intricate consultant-client system can be made simpler by strategically grouping the various entities into three categories (Cockman, Evans, & Reynolds, 1992):

- *Those who know:* They are aware of the problem(s) to be confronted.
- *Those who care:* They suffer from the problem(s) afflicting the enterprise.
- *Those who can:* They are the sponsors of the consulting assignment and have the power to green light the improvement project.

Each of these groups has an important role to play and a stake in the consulting collaboration. The outcome will be poorer if a consultant actively engages *those who know* and *those who care* without listening to *those who can*.

Navigating the co-active relationship

Objective advice from a consultant is sought by clients for various reasons. For instance, the client may need an expert to discover and/or fix a particular problem, enhance learning, or require assistance to put into action some talking points, or necessitate the services of an organizational "interpreter" to re-interpret a problematic issue and to provide meaning for other organizational members, or help make sense of various organizational events. Regardless of the reason for tapping into an outside consultant, the client firm should follow these five steps:

- *Step 1:* Explain what is *really* going on. If you can, go to Step 2. If you cannot, go to Step 3.
- *Step 2:* Try to resolve the problem *without* hiring consultants. Explore other options; for example, invite a retired senior executive to help out. If this is not possible, go to Step 3.
- *Step 3:* Hire a professional consultant to help and advise.

- *Step 4*: Decide on the project extension, recycling, or termination criteria.
- *Step 5*: Own the solution.

Cementing a successful client-consultant relationship involves extensive navigation. Because of project freezes, stormy developments and shifting winds, sands and currents and the possibility of tsunami, there is no guarantee that the final destination will be that which was originally imagined or intended. The process is said to be similar to cycling through four seasons (Mulligan & Barber, 2001), namely:

- *The people-centered Orientation Season*: the spring of the client-consultant relationship, when the client and consultant are first introduced to each other, and when their needs and expectations begin to materialize and the ground rules and trust between the two parties are developed and begin to grow and flower.
- *The problem-centered Identification Season*: the summer of the relationship, when the scope of work is agreed on, problems are clarified, work on the project is underway and the endeavor meets with sweet zephyrs or August storms, but it is evident that the fruits of the effort are soon to be picked.
- *The strategy-centered Explorations Season*: the autumn of the relationship, when chosen strategies are executed, the fruit is plucked from the vine, and the bad apples are culled.
- *The results-centered Resolution Season*: the winter of the client-consultant relationship, when the delivered project is evaluated and all those concerned are debriefed to capture their insights and we see Christmas and New Year's Eve and hopefully, no hang-over.

The building blocks of a harmonious relationship

Consulting has also been compared to a highly dynamic and frequently turbulent contact sport (e.g., Czerniawska, 2007; Fincham, 1999; Fullerton & West, 1996; Glückler & Armbrüster, 2003; Heizmann, 2011; Karantinou & Hogg, 2001; Levina & Orlikowski, 2009; Mohe & Seidl, 2011; Orr & Orr, 2013). To create and sustain a positive, authentic, and value-adding partnership in any consulting assignment and to keep the puck on the ice, six building blocks are recommended.

Building block 1: tap organizational social capital

Social capital is the best means for importing external advice and knowledge into a firm. Developing organizational social capital requires grasping hold of the knowledge and information assets found in a firm's human resources and in its formal and informal/social networks with outsiders (customers, affiliates, and connected employees of other firms or of the government) (Anand, Glick & Manz, 2002).

Building block 2: inquire humbly

In the problem-solving environment of contemporary businesses, consultants have grown used to arrogantly telling instead of asking, and doing so especially not in a humble way. *Telling* may make others feel as though they are being put down; *asking* will empower them. An engagement in which consultants do less telling and more asking and acknowledging creates a high-quality partnership that is balanced and sociologically equitable (Schein, 2013).

Building block 3: create a respectful engagement that conveys a sense of worth

To this end, there are five strategies: being fully present; being genuine; communicating affirmation; listening effectively; and offering supportive communication (Dutton, 2003).

Building block 4: facilitate another person's successful performance

Five galvanizing actions to take that enable staff members to successfully address the tasks at hand are: teaching; designing; advocating; accommodating; and nurturing (Dutton, 2003).

Building block 5: develop trust

According to Dutton (2003), you can build up trust by what you say (e.g., share some new facts about yourself); by what you do *not* say (do not blame your business partners for ill will or discredit them); by what you do (empower partnership and try delegating more tasks); and by what you do *not* do (do not disparage people and their achievements).

Building block 6: be mindful and have meaningful fun

Consulting is serious business and hard work indeed. Nevertheless, there is real value in transcending what seems at times mundane, dreary, mind-numbing drudgery by injecting some meaningful fun into consulting assignments (Huy, 2005). One strategy is to devote some time each assignment day (between business meetings, while commuting – whenever there is a free moment) to engage in, say, a contemplative, loving-kindness meditation practice. By mindfully contemplating those who are closest to you, such as family or project team members, and meditating on the good qualities they have shared with you, you will become calmer and more deeply connected to life, without sacrificing productivity. In these times of 24/7 connectivity, multitasking, and instant messaging, mindfulness and meaningful fun are the antidote to unwanted distractions and extreme stress.

The top five qualities of a professional consultant

To deliver on the promise of providing high-quality, ethical, and expert advisory services, a consultant must hold or work on developing the following key qualities:

- *Consulting skills*: These include in-depth knowledge of value-adding performance consulting cycles and processes (from pre-entry, entry, and contracting, through design, development, delivery, program close, and post-engagement learning). Moreover, they embody insight into research-led practice and practice-led research, consultancy and research techniques, scientific management methods and models (strategic, tactical, and operational), risk management, positive organizational change leadership, design, program and project management. Professional qualifications include a Master's degree in HRD and consultancy, a Master's degree in management consultancy and organizational change, an education in OD, and/or a specialized Master of Business Administration (MBA) in (HRD/OD) consulting.
- *In-depth business expertise*: This embraces not only functional and industry expertise, but also insight into the client's specific business.
- *Personal effectiveness*: The consultant should manifest a commitment to being helpful, humble in inquiry, caring, emotionally resilient, and positive in manner and communication. Ideally, he or she should also have a winning mindset, genuine curiosity, and the ability to successfully navigate the Scylla and Charybdis of complexity and ambiguity; be accountable, authentic, analytical, entrepreneurial, and resourceful; have good team and people skills, and be able to build and sustain client relationships and ultimately to elevate themselves to *trusted advisor* status; use integrative and design thinking; be effective in negotiating genuinely and managing difficult conversations; know how to efficiently organize and prioritize tasks; and be driven and able to travel frequently and adhere to extremely tight deadlines.
- *Learning agility*: This requires dedication to continuous learning and to never-ending professional development.
- *Ethics*: The consultant's behavior should be guided by ethical decision-making, integrity, and adherence to a code of professional conduct.

Increase in the credibility of a consultant comes through rigorous consulting and ongoing demonstration of their practical contribution and long-term value to the business client and to organizational performance. Should these be met, the consultant will show true value and their professional practice will flourish.

The heart of effective consulting: co-creating value

Although the insights presented here are a mere slice of real-world consulting experiences and dynamics, they do lay the positive, viable groundwork on which strategic and results-driven HRD/OD consulting work can develop. While giving central stage to the value of the various elements of high-level consulting, the experiences of the insurance company that were shared in the case study can also serve to fuel further education on the integration of consulting theory and practice. The event took place, albeit there was more to the story than that recounted here.

Ultimately, the foundation of consultancy is the co-creation of value so that the client's condition and performance are enhanced. In consulting work, the assignment is successful only if the client is demonstrably better off after the engagement. This improvement can take myriad forms, among them: optimizing the workplace in support of the business goal; improving organizational efficiency; solving a difficult human or organizational performance problem; jump-starting a positive organizational change or a learning program; uncovering previously untapped sources of organization, effectiveness and health; energizing the workplace; enhancing the knowledge base; raising the quality of management dialogue; making sure that strategic decisions and recommendations are driven by data and based on evidence; reinterpreting a complex issue so that it can be properly addressed; providing the language needed to facilitate organizational reform; transferring critical skills; tracking management trends; finding the sources of friction to the betterment of the entity; promoting and sharing next-practice thought leadership; controlling costs; and crafting a winning talent and organization development strategy.

None of these goals can be reached, however, without the equal and enthusiastic participation and partnership of both client and consultant. The two together make an unbeatable team, but if the two are not singing from the same hymn sheet, the result is death metal, not high opera.

Summary propositions

Recap and revise the key takeaways from the chapter:

- In Chapter 2, the underlying tenets of the *dialogic* organization development (OD) approach to leading positive change and engagement were demonstrated. In this chapter, to capture its full potential, it is exemplified how a comprehensive and systematic *diagnostic* OD can be strategically integrated with a really good dialogic OD to create an effective change process. The *diagnostic-dialogic* extension of the OD approach to change is particularly successful in a VUCA world of continual change – it positions *positive* OD optimally to be able to impact how change in enterprises is led and executed.

- Love it or hate it, *management consulting* is an alluring yet misunderstood profession. In seeking to increase revenues, maximize efficiency, and control costs, demand for professional design and transition consulting services continues to grow – worldwide.
- *Practical rigor* is needed to establish a sound foundation for strategic and results-driven human resource development (HRD) and organization development (OD) consulting work.
- To yield the reliable *intelligence* vital to support strategic HR and OD decisions, consultants need to juggle a strong grounding in scientific research techniques with their creative application.
- Any results-driven HRD consultancy effort starts with appreciating the three core domains of strategically integrated and deliverables-oriented HRD: *organizational learning, organizational performance*, and *organizational change*.
- The experiences of a global insurance company seeking to revamp its rigid training function into an agile learning and development (L&D) one serves to highlight the value of powerful consulting guidance in the science and art of designing and building a knowledge-creative environment, and in *strategically aligning* L&D with the full development of the organization's overall strategy. The avenue to *positive* strategic transformation that was ultimately selected was to adopt the ERG model – methodologically and experimentally. It helped to experiment with, seed, and catalyze change.
- Although transformational change is *not* quick, ERG is a powerful method for leading and executing *generative* change. It upsets the traditional OD approach to organizational change, and it breathes fresh air into how we think about OD and change. Yet, it requires quite a bit of whole organization work, big picture thinking, and doing integrated organization design management and development.
- *Organization design* is more than another "reorg." It is part and parcel of the strategy of OD. When one does strategy separately from design, one will eventually end up with a great deal of misalignment.
- A comprehensive review of the myriad aspects of *modern consulting practice* in building a positive framework for business leaders and theorists serves to illustrate how issues are tackled in real-life business situations, and to enable safe navigation through the key facets of this highly competitive and demanding profession.

Acknowledgments

This chapter builds and expands on "A Balanced Approach to Professional HRD Consulting: Lessons from the Field" by B. Tkaczyk in *Global Business and Organizational Excellence* 36(4), 2017. Copyright © 2017 Wiley Periodicals, Inc. The author is grateful to the publisher of the journal for licensing back to the author the right to reuse the published contribution for book publication. Also, the author thanks Mary Ann Castronovo Fusco for her helpful comments on an earlier version.

References for further reading

Academy of Human Resource Development (AHRD). (2020). Retrieved from: www. ahrd.org

Acquisdata. (2019). *Acquisdata global industry snapshot: Management consulting industry*. Wilmington, DE: Acquisdata Inc.

Anand, V., Glick, W., & Manz, C. (2002). Thriving on the knowledge of outsiders: Tapping organizational social capital. *The Academy of Management Executive*, 16(1), 87–101.

Association for Talent Development (ATD). (2016a). *Building a culture of learning: The foundation of a successful organization*. Alexandria, VA: Association for Talent Development.

Association for Talent Development (ATD). (2016b). *Evaluating learning: Getting to measurements that matter*. Alexandria, VA: Association for Talent Development.

Association for Talent Development (ATD). (2020). Retrieved from: www.td.org

ASTD (American Society for Training & Development). (1980). HRD consulting – Should you or shouldn't you? *Training and Development Journal*, 34(4), 80–91.

Austin, R., & Devin, L. (2003). *Artful making: What managers need to know about how artists work*. Upper Saddle River, NJ: Financial Times Prentice Hall.

Bahrami, H., & Evans, S. (2010). *Super-flexibility for knowledge enterprises: A toolkit for dynamic adaptation*. Heidelberg, Germany: Springer.

Bahrami, H., & Evans S. (2011). Super-flexibility for real-time adaptation: Perspectives from Silicon Valley. *California Management Review*, 53(3), 21–39.

Becker, G. (1964). *Human capital*. New York, NY: Columbia University Press.

Becker, G. (1993). Nobel lecture: The economic way of looking at behavior. *The Journal of Political Economy*, 101(3), 385–409.

Berglund, J., & Werr, A. (2000). The invincible character of management consulting rhetoric: How one blends incommensurates while keeping them apart. *Organization*, 7(4), 633–655.

BLS (Bureau of Labor Statistics) (2019). *Occupational outlook handbook: Management analysts*. Washington, DC: Bureau of Labor Statistics, U.S. Department of Labor.

Boland, R., & Collopy, F. (Eds.). (2004). *Managing as designing*. Stanford, CA: Stanford University Press.

Brown, T. (2009). *Change by design: How design thinking transforms organizations and inspires innovation*. New York, NY: HarperBusiness.

Burack, E. (1991). Changing the company culture: The role of human resource development. *Long Range Planning*, 24(1), 88–95.

Caldwell, R. (2003). The changing roles of personnel managers: Old ambiguities, new uncertainties. *Journal of Management Studies*, 40(4), 983–1004.

Caldwell, R. (2008). HR business partner competency models: Re-contextualising effectiveness. *Human Resource Management Journal*, 18(3), 275–294.

Cameron, K., Dutton, J., & Quinn, R. (Eds.). (2003). *Positive organizational scholarship: Foundations of a new discipline*. San Francisco, CA: Berrett-Koehler.

Cameron, K., & Spreitzer, G. (Eds.). (2012). *The Oxford handbook of positive organizational scholarship*. New York, NY: Oxford University Press.

Cascio, W., & Boudreau, J. (2015). *Investing in people: Financial impact of human resource initiatives* (2nd ed.). Upper Saddle River, NJ: FT Press.

CIPD (Chartered Institute of Personnel and Development). (2004). *Business partnering: A new direction for HR*. London, UK: Chartered Institute of Personnel and Development.

CIPD (Chartered Institute of Personnel and Development). (2016). *HR outlook, Winter 2015–16: Leaders' views of our profession*. London, UK: Chartered Institute of Personnel and Development.

CIPD (Chartered Institute of Personnel and Development). (2020). Retrieved from: www.cipd.co.uk

Clark, T. (1995). *Managing consultants: Consultancy as the management of impressions*. Buckingham, UK: Open University Press.

Clark, T., & Fincham, R. (2002). *Critical consulting: New perspectives on the management advice industry*. Oxford, UK: Blackwell.

Clark, T., & Salaman, G. (1998a). Creating the "right" impression: Towards a dramaturgy of management consultancy. *The Service Industries Journal*, 18(1), 18–38.

Clark, T., & Salaman, G. (1998b). Telling tales: Management gurus' narratives and the construction of managerial identity. *The Journal of Management Studies*, 35(2), 137–161.

Clegg, S., Kornberger, M., & Rhodes, C. (2004). Noise, parasites and translation: Theory and practice in management consulting. *Management Learning*, 35(1), 31–44.

CMC-Canada. (2016). *Management consulting in Canada: 2016 industry report*. Toronto, Canada: The Canadian Association of Management Consultants.

CMR. (2020). Special issue on design thinking. *California Management Review*, 62(2).

Cockman, P., Evans, B., & Reynolds, P. (1992). *Client-centred consulting: A practical guide for internal advisers and trainers*. London, UK: McGraw-Hill.

Collins, D. (2004). Who put the con in consultancy? Fads, recipes and "vodka margarine." *Human Relations*, 57(5), 553–572.

Consultancy.Asia (2018). Asia Pacific management consulting industry breaks $50 billion barrier. Amsterdam: consultancy.org.

Craig, D. (2005). *Rip-off! The scandalous inside story of the management consulting money machine*. London, UK: Original Book Co.

CRF. (2009). *The effective HR business partner*. London, UK: Corporate Research Forum.

Czerniawska, F. (2007). *The trusted firm: How consulting firms build successful client relationships*. Chichester: Wiley.

DMI Review. (2015). Organization development and design management. *DMI Review*, 26(3).

Dutton, J. (2003). *Energize your workplace: How to create and sustain high-quality connections at work*. San Francisco, CA: Jossey-Bass.

Fincham, R. (1999). The consultant–client relationship: Critical perspectives on the management of organizational change. *Journal of Management Studies*, 36(30), 335–351.

Fincham, R. (2000). Management as magic: Reengineering and the search for business salvation. In D. Knights & H. Willmott (Eds.), *The reengineering revolution: Critical studies of corporate change* (pp. 174–191). London, UK: Sage.

Francis, H., & Keegan, A. (2006). The changing face of HRM: In search of balance. *Human Resource Management Journal*, 16(3), 231–249.

Fullerton, J., & West, M. (1996). Consultant and client: Working together? *Journal of Managerial Psychology*, 11(6), 40–49.

Gilley, J., & Gilley, A. (2003). *Strategically integrated HRD* (2nd ed.). Cambridge, MA: Perseus.

Glückler, J., & Armbrüster, T. (2003). Bridging uncertainty in management consulting: The mechanisms of trust and networked reputation. *Organization Studies*, 24(2), 269–297.

Gross, A., & Poor, J. (2008). The global management consulting sector. *Business Economics*, 43(4), 59–68.

Guest, D. (1987). Human resource management and industrial relations. *Journal of Management Studies*, 24(5), 503–521.

Hall, D. (1984). Human resource development and organizational effectiveness. In C. Fombrun, N. Tichy, & M. Devanna (Eds.), *Strategic human resource management* (pp. 159–182). New York, NY: Wiley.

Heizmann, H. (2011). Knowledge sharing in a dispersed network of HR practice: Zooming in on power/knowledge struggles. *Management Learning*, 42(4), 379–393.

Heusinkveld, S., & Benders, J. (2005). Contested commodification: Consultancies and their struggle with new concept development. *Human Relations*, 58(3), 283–310.

Hope-Hailey, V., Farndale, E., & Truss, C. (2005). The HR department's role in organizational performance. *Human Resource Management Journal*, 15(3), 49–66.

Huy, Q. (2005). An emotion-based view of strategic renewal. In G. Szulanski, J. Porac, & Y. Doz (Eds.), *Strategy process: Advances in strategic management* (vol. 22, pp. 3–37). Bingley, UK: Emerald.

Jacobs, R. (1997). HRD partnerships for integrating HRD research and practice. In R. Swanson & E. Holton III (Eds.), *Human resource development research handbook: Linking research and practice* (pp. 47–61). San Francisco, CA: Berrett-Koehler.

Jamieson, D. (2015). Q&A: David Jamieson. *Design Management Review*, 26(3), 9–12.

Kantola, A., & Seeck, H. (2011). Dissemination of management into politics: Michael Porter and the political uses of management consulting. *Management Learning*, 42(1), 25–47.

Karantinou, K., & Hogg, M. (2001). Exploring relationship management in professional services: A study of management consultancy. *Journal of Marketing Management*, 17(3/4), 263–286.

Kieser, A. (2002). Managers as marionettes? Using fashion theories to explain the success of consultancies. In M. Kipping & L. Engwall (Eds.), *Management consulting: An emerging knowledge industry* (pp. 167–183). Oxford, UK: Oxford University Press.

King, N., & Anderson, N. (2020). *Managing innovation and change: A critical guide for organizations*. London, UK: Thompson.

Kipping, M., & Clark, T. (2012). *The Oxford handbook of management consulting*, New York, NY: Oxford University Press.

Levina, N., & Orlikowski, W. (2009). Understanding shifting power relations within and across organizations: A critical genre analysis. *Academy of Management Journal*, 52(4), 672–703.

Lockwood, T. (Ed.) (2009). *Design thinking: Integrating innovation, customer experience, and brand value*. New York, NY: Allworth Press.

Management Consultancies Association (MCA). (2016). *The definitive guide to UK consulting industry statistics 2016*. London, UK: Management Consultancies Association.

Martin, R. (2009). *The design of business: Why design thinking is the next competitive advantage*. Boston, MA: Harvard Business Press.

Mohe, M., & Seidl, D. (2011). Theorizing the client–consultant relationship from the perspective of social-systems theory. *Organization*, 18(1), 3–22.

Mulligan, J., & Barber, P. (2001). The client-consultant relationship. In P. Sadler (Ed.), *Management consultancy: A handbook for best practice* (2nd ed., pp. 66–85). London, UK: Kogan Page.

Nadler, L. (1970). *Developing human resources*. Houston, TX: Gulf.

Organization Development Network (OD Network). (2020). Retrieved from: www.odnetwork.org

Orr, L., & Orr, D. (2013). *When to hire or not hire a consultant: Getting your money's worth from consulting relationships*. New York, NY: Apress.

Phelan, K. (2013). *I'm sorry I broke your company: When management consultants are the problem, not the solution*. San Francisco, CA: Berrett-Koehler.

Pickard, J. (2005). Part, not partner. *People Management*, 11(21), 48–50.

Reilly, P., & Williams, T. (2006). *Strategic HR: Building the capability to deliver*. London. UK: Gower.

Saint-Martin, D. (2004). *Building the new managerialist state: Consultants and the politics of public sector reform in comparative perspective*. Oxford, UK: Oxford University Press.

Schein, E. (1987). *Process consultation: Lessons for managers and consultants* (vol. 2). Reading, MA: Addison-Wesley.

Schein, E. (1997). The concept of "client" from a process consultation perspective: A guide for change agents. *Journal of Organizational Change Management*, 10(3), 202–216.

Schein, E. (2013). *Humble inquiry: The gentle art of asking instead of telling*. San Francisco, CA: Berrett-Koehler.

Schultz, T. (1961). Investment in human capital. *American Economic Review*, 51(1), 1–17.

Source Global Research. (2018a). *Perceptions of consulting in the UK*. London, UK: Source Information Services Ltd.

Source Global Research. (2018b). *The Eastern Europe consulting market in 2018*. London, UK: Source Information Services Ltd.

Source Global Research. (2018c). *The Russia consulting market in 2018*. London, UK: Source Information Services Ltd.

Source Global Research. (2018d). *The Australia consulting market in 2018*. London, UK: Source Information Services Ltd.

Source Global Research. (2018e). *The China consulting market in 2018*. London, UK: Source Information Services Ltd.

Source Global Research. (2019a). *The US consulting market in 2019*. London, UK: Source Information Services Ltd.

Source Global Research. (2019b). *The Eastern Europe & Russia consulting market in 2019*. London, UK: Source Information Services Ltd.

Source Global Research. (2019c). *The Australia consulting market in 2019*. London, UK: Source Information Services Ltd.

Source Global Research. (2019d). *The Japan consulting market in 2019*. London, UK: Source Information Services Ltd.

Source Global Research. (2019e). *The India consulting market in 2019*. London, UK: Source Information Services Ltd.

Source Global Research. (2019f). *The China consulting market in 2019*. London, UK: Source Information Services Ltd.

Source Global Research. (2019g). *The GCC consulting market in 2019*. London, UK: Source Information Services Ltd.

Source Global Research. (2020a). *The UK consulting market in 2020*. London, UK: Source Information Services Ltd.

Source Global Research. (2020b). *The GCC consulting market in 2020*. London, UK: Source Information Services Ltd.

Statistics Canada. (2019). *Consulting services: Summary statistics; Sales by type of client; Breakdown of sales*. Ottawa, Canada: Statistics Canada.

Sturdy, A., Clark, T., Fincham, R., & Handley, K. (2009). Between innovation and legitimation: Boundaries and knowledge flow in management consultancy. *Organization*, 16(5), 627–653.

Tkaczyk, B. (2015a). Leading as constant learning and development: The knowledge-creative enterprise. *Design Management Review*, 26(3), 38–43.

Tkaczyk, B. (2015b). Strategizing to win on the global playing field: Making real strategic choices in people operations. *European Business Review*, Sept/Oct, 64–69.

Tkaczyk, B. (2018). Business leadership for the management consulting industry: A new model for the greater good. *Rutgers Business Review*, 3(1), 53–66.

Wright, P., McMahan, G., & McWilliams, A. (1994). Human resources and sustained competitive advantage: A resource-based perspective. *The International Journal of Human Resource Management*, 5(2), 301–326.

Part II

ToolBox

Tools and templates for the practice of leading *positive* organizational change

The ToolBox contents

Tools and templates for the practice of leading positive organizational change

ToolBox	15 dynamic actions	30 tools, worksheets and exercises		
ENERGIZE WorkBox	**E1.** Diagnose for change, including undertaking a pre-change audit of the system-wide fitness for organizational change, as well as an inquiry into organizational memory, and experience of past change initiatives	ERG Organizational Change ScoreCard	Organizational Fitness for Change Audit	Pressure Meter
	E2. Awaken by building a compelling case for change, as well as by evangelizing the change purpose, touching and connecting with people by means of storytelling and collaborative and generative "change conversations"	Crafting a Signature Story that F.I.R.E.S.!	Seeing Is Doing	
	E3. Mobilize resources and find strengths	Big 4 Leadership Ways: Self-Assessment Inventory	Continuing Self-coaching: Becoming a Corporate Olympian	
	E4. Select and engage positive culture-fit "change energizers"	Positive Workplace Culture Fit		
	E5. Socialize and empathize with others and with the workplace environment as a whole	Positive Workplace Cultural Assets Audit	Fun@Work	

REDESIGN WorkBox		Sunnier Side of Life Search	Picture It!	I.M.A.G.I.N.E.R. Innovation Booster
	R1. Co-craft the "sunnier side of life" in strategic collaboration with organizational members and stakeholders, by way of collective design thinking and appreciative future search (*What is already working well? What if anything were possible? What exactly wows? What happens to that, if we do this?*)	Sunnier Side of Life Search	Picture It!	I.M.A.G.I.N.E.R. Innovation Booster
	R2. Remodel organizational structure, processes, and components, if necessary	Optimizer		
	R3. Navigate and manage power and politics, resistance, a change coalition (e.g., a dedicated "design team") and core business	Strategic Stakeholder Ecosystem Navigator	Quick and Positive Comebacks	
	R4. Coach and develop for positive leadership, engagement, and organizational renewal	Coach's Self-Check	Coaching Conversations To G.R.O.W.	
	R5. Before roll-out, run disciplined learning launches to de-risk change initiative execution	Disciplined Learning Launches		

(Continued)

Tools and templates for the practice of leading positive organizational change

ToolBox	15 dynamic actions	30 tools, worksheets and exercises		
GEL WorkBox	**G1.** Continuously model, monitor, and measure progress and performance, basing decisions upon metrics chosen in an open book way	Progress, Performance and Impact Traffic Light System		
	G2. Reward and celebrate quick wins	Gamifying Quick Wins	Crafting Success Challenge	Philharmonic Symphony Orchestra: Marching to Victory
	G3. Integrate change lessons learned	Know-How Assets Transfer		
	G4. Reinforce and sustain the organization's new state	Built to Change	Total Reward Mix: Developing Reward Strategies	Job Re-Imagined
	G5. Keep strategizing to win, and keep self-regenerating through continuous, experiential, social and reflective learning, self-organizing, designing, experimenting, and innovating (including practicing *open* innovation via crowdsourcing, innovation intermediaries, or open innovation software)	Leader's Developmental Portfolio: Continuing Executive Development	Trend-Spotter	

4   The Energize WorkBox

10 tools

The Energize WorkBox contents

Energize				
ToolBox	*Dynamic actions*	*Tools, worksheets and exercises*		
ENERGIZE WorkBox	**E1.** Diagnose for change, including undertaking a prechange audit of the system-wide fitness for organizational change, as well as an inquiry into organizational memory, and experience of past change initiatives	ERG Organizational Change Scorecard	Organizational Fitness for Change Audit	Pressure Meter
	E2. Awaken by building a compelling case for change, as well as by evangelizing the change purpose, touching and connecting with people by means of storytelling and collaborative and generative "change conversations"	Crafting a Signature Story that F.I.R.E.S.!	Seeing Is Doing	
	E3. Mobilize resources and find strengths	Big 4 Leadership Ways: Self-Assessment Inventory	Continuing Self-coaching: Becoming a Corporate Olympian	
	E4. Select and engage positive culture-fit "change energizers"	Positive Workplace Culture Fit		
	E5. Socialize and empathize with others and with the workplace environment as a whole	Positive Workplace Cultural Assets Audit	Fun@Work	

ERG organizational change scorecard

Are you the key that will open the door to positive change? Let's find out!
Use Table E1.1 and then Table E1.2.

Table E1.1 ERG organizational change scorecard

	Energize – Redesign – Gel (ERG) positive organizational change self-assessment scorecard	Almost never	Rarely	Sometimes	Often	Constantly
Stage	***As a change leader, assess yourself to see to what extent you:***	1	2	3	4	5
Energize	**E1.** Diagnose for change, do a pre-change audit of the system-wide fitness for organizational change, inquire into organizational memory and experience of past change initiatives. Find out if change is wanted and accepted and why or why not					
	E2. Awaken by building a compelling case for change, as well as by evangelizing the change purpose, touching and connecting with people by means of storytelling and collaborative "change conversations"					
	E3. Mobilize resources and find strengths					
	E4. Select and engage positive culture-fit "change energizers"					
	E5. Socialize and empathize with others and with the workplace environment as a whole					
	TOTAL for E. ENERGIZE (Add together the values):					_____ / 25
Reflective notes						
Redesign	**R1.** Co-craft the "positive" – the "sunnier side of life" in strategic collaboration with organizational members and stakeholders, by way of collective design thinking and appreciative future search (*What is already working well? What if anything were possible? What exactly wows? What exactly works?*)					
	R2. Remodel organizational structure, processes and components, if necessary					
	R3. Navigate and manage power and politics, resistance, and pro-/anti-change coalitions (e.g., by putting into place a dedicated "design team"), while maintaining core business					

Energize – Redesign – Gel (ERG) positive organizational change self-assessment scorecard	Almost never	Rarely	Sometimes	Often	Constantly
Stage — *As a change leader, assess yourself to see to what extent you:*	1	2	3	4	5

Stage						
Redesign	**R4.** Coach and develop for positive leadership and engagement (find the right people, enable them to make effective the intended change)					
	R5. Before roll-out, run disciplined learning launches – to de-risk change initiative execution by seeing what works, what does not, what is acceptable and in what time period					
	TOTAL for R. REDESIGN (Add together the values):					_____ / 25
Reflective notes						
Gel	**G1.** Constantly model, monitor, and measure progress and performance – basing decisions on metrics chosen in an open-book way, above board, not concealed					
	G2. Reward and celebrate quick wins					
	G3. Integrate change lessons learned					
	G4. Reinforce and sustain the organization's new state					
	G5. Keep strategizing to win, and keep self-regenerating through continuous, experiential, social and reflective learning, self-organizing, designing, experimenting, and innovating (including practicing *open* innovation via crowdsourcing, innovation intermediaries, or open innovation software)					
	TOTAL for G. GEL (Add together the values):					_____ / 25
Reflective notes						
	GRAND TOTAL (E + R + G):					_____ / 75

Guide to scores

1 = your change leadership performance is deficient and requires upgrading.
2 = your change leadership performance is barely sufficient and requires upgrading.
3 = your change leadership performance is generally satisfactory but may require upgrading.
4 = your change leadership performance is above average but not great in every respect.
5 = your change leadership performance is excellent.

Change outcome: 0–36 Deficient; 37–44 Sporadic; 45–52 Needs Improvement; 53–63 Above Average; 64–75 Extremely Good.

Try filling in Table E1.2.

Table E1.2 ERG scorecard continued

Change project scheme				
What will you do to energize the workplace and boost employee experience and engagement? Log efforts	*Scope/ spec*	*Cost/ resources*	*Time to produce a deliverable/ schedule*	*Success metrics/ expected outcomes*
Run a strategy imagination forum to develop moonshot ambition and goals				
Co-create an energizing purpose statement				
Codify defining leadership principles				
Scale a peer-to-peer global community				
What needs redesigning?	*Scope/ Spec*	*Cost/ resources*	*Time to produce a deliverable/ schedule*	*Success metrics/ expected outcomes*
Strategy (vision, direction, competitive advantage)				
Structure (power and authority, reporting relationships, organizational roles)				
Reward systems (goals, scorecards and metrics, compensation)				
Talent management and development practices (staffing and selection, diversity, performance feedback, learning and development)				
Symbols, rituals, and routines				
List actions you will take to improve	*Scope/ spec*	*Cost/ resources*	*Time to produce a deliverable/ schedule*	*Success metrics/ expected outcomes*
Model, monitor and measure change progress and performance				

Celebrate wins

Integrate the change lessons learned

Reinforce and sustain change

Keep self-regenerating

Organizational fitness for change audit

Want to find out if your enterprise is ready for change? For each organizational fitness area, in Table E1.3, rate your organizational strength by marking H (High), M (Medium), L (Low), or N (nonexistent). First, complete it individually. Next, hold an executive leadership team meeting to discuss scoring.

Table E1.3 Organizational fitness for change (ORGFIT-24) audit

Organizational fitness for change factor (ORGFIT-24)	*Rating*
1. Executive sponsorship	
2. Active and positive leadership	
3. Evidence-based management	
4. Change drive and energy	
5. Clear purpose, winning aspirations, and moonshot goals	
6. Market space research	
7. High-quality links between organizational strategy and functional strategies	
8. Nimble organizational structure and design	
9. Technology and performance metrics	
10. Customer-centeredness	
11. Consulting internal and external stakeholders	
12. Employee engagement, health, voice, and well-being	
13. Talent and diversity management, and resourcing	
14. Reward package and incentive schemes	
15. Constant coaching, (reverse) mentoring, and development	
16. Positive organizational culture	

(Continued)

Organizational fitness for change factor (ORGFIT-24)	*Rating*

17. Knowledge management and transfer

18. Learning from disciplined experiments and (open) innovation execution

19. Design thinking and applied imagination

20. Ethical principles

21. High morale and high-quality human connections, including support from those who are impacted by the change

22. Trust

23. Right timing and effort (to avoid excessive change and initiative fatigue)

24. History of change (positive record of change leadership)

TOTAL RANKING

Guide to scores
Give 3 points for H
Give 2 points for M
Give 1 point for L
Give 0 point for N
Total ranking: _____

Fitness Rating and Advice

Level 72–56: fit and ready for change

Change outcomes can be achieved. Positive change will be a result of planned action. To boost the change process, "energize" the workplace and allocate resources to lagging dimensions (Ls, Ms, and Ns).

Level 55–39: somewhat fit and ready for change

Some, but not all, change intentions are achievable. Change may need to be modified again after it is initially implemented. To produce intentional change outcomes, address pressures (internal/external), (conflicting) interests, power, different skills levels of personnel. Likewise, better manage lagging areas (deal with Ls, Ms, and Ns), and "plus energize" the workplace and, if necessary, re-design strategies, systems, structures, roles, protocols, practices, and policies.

Level 0–38: unfit and unready for change

Sorry ... change outcomes will not be achieved. Pressures (internal/external) are beyond your control. The organization is not yet ready for change, and any change initiative will fail. To remedy, first institute (new/nonexistent) strategies, systems, structures, roles, protocols, practices, and policies. Continue to energize and re-design. For the moment, implementing change, at any rate, might lead the organization to catastrophe, so back off and set the stage for change.

Routine

This audit is for use with an executive leadership team. Come back to this instrument and apply it again and again so as to identify progress as change is phased in, and to know when change will take off and fly!

Further notes

Make some notes for change.

_____

_____

_____

Pressure meter

Measure the current pressures for change in Table E1.4. What's going to pump it up? What's going to let the air out?

Table E1.4 Pressure meter

Pressures for change/relative strength	Very weak	Weak	Neutral	Strong	Very strong
Internal (organizational) sources	*1*	*2*	*3*	*4*	*5*
History of change (the effect of a bad track record of change management)					
Absence/presence of organizational fitness for change					
Culture (organizational)					
Identity					
Resources					
New broom					
Departmental power/inter-unit politics					
Employee well-being					
Growth					
...					

(Continued)

External (environmental) sources	*1*	*2*	*3*	*4*	*5*
Economy (shifts in economic factors)					
Geopolitical/investors' risks/military actions					
Public health/epidemics/pandemics					
Threat of new entrants/substitutes					
Bargaining power of buyers/suppliers					
Demographics/human migration/birth and death rates/income					
Environment/extreme weather conditions					
(Social) media/telecommunications/5G					
Fashions/fads					
Government/legal/taxation/elections					
…					

Analyze the pressures to make decisions as regards implementation of change. Consider both "restraining" pressures (= pushing against change initiative execution) as well as "energizing" forces (= driving forward change initiative execution) (Figure E1.1).

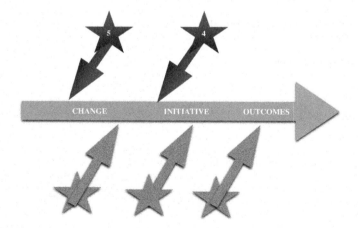

Figure E1.1 Pressure meter

Map the organization and environment of today and forecast tomorrow's in Table E1.5 Pressures and organizational responses.

Table E1.5 Pressures and organizational responses

Pressure-sourced demands	Organizational dynamic responses
Internal (organization)	
External (environment)	

Crafting a signature story that F.I.R.E.S.!

Reflect

1. Why do people in all cultures like to tell or listen to stories? Do you prefer telling stories or listening to them?
2. What makes an extremely good story? What makes an extremely good storyteller? Do you know anybody who is a fantastic storyteller? What kind of stories does (s)he tell?
3. Close your eyes and think back to your childhood and think of stories that your (grand)parents/teachers told you or read to you. How universal are they?
4. What common forms of storytelling are there in today's society?
5. When did you last hear an extremely good business story? What was it about?
6. In your own words, tell the stories of:

Robin Hood

_____

_____

_____

Enron

_____

_____

_____

Figure E2.1 Signature story

Everybody needs a signature story that F.I.R.E.S. (Fresh, Informative, Re-lated, Energizing/Evangelical, Strategic). What's yours? Tell your signature story now (Figure E2.1).

Craft your signature story that F.I.R.E.S.

Note all the ingredients of an extremely good story in Table E2.1. Ensure that your signature story/business narrative F.I.R.E.S.

Table E2.1 Crafting a signature story that F.I.R.E.S!

Signature storytelling that F.I.R.E.S.

5 Cornerstones	25 Defining characteristics	Check box
FRESH	1. Does it have a fresh focus/goal?	_____
	2. Is it cool/funny?	_____
	3. Is it different?	_____
	4. Is it original?	_____
	5. Is it radical?	_____
INFORMATIVE	1. Does it give useful information, as well as stand out as a message in these overloaded/distorted/ambiguous and noisy times?	_____
	2. Is it memorable, meaningful, visual, and rich in sensory imagery (e.g. precise, vivid vocabulary, descriptive details, metaphors/comparisons, smells, tastes, onomatopoeia)?	_____
	3. Does it provide a moral/comment?	_____
	4. Does it add detail/impact?	_____
	5. Is it conversational as well as instructive?	_____

Signature storytelling that F.I.R.E.S.

5 Cornerstones	25 Defining characteristics	Check box
RELATED	1. Can the audience relate to the story? Is it personal, authentic, and vulnerable?	_____
	2. Is it applicable?	_____
	3. Should the audience care? Is it closely connected with their values and appropriate to the matter at hand?	_____
	4. Does it touch and make them listen and connect with you?	_____
	5. Does it develop a positive personal/emotional reaction, collaboration, or positive followership?	_____
ENERGIZING/ EVANGELICAL	1. Does it boost vitality, enthusiasm, hope, and awakening? Does it communicate who you are and who the company is?	_____
	2. Does it empower and energize people to act?	_____
	3. Does it build and sustain high-quality connections?	_____
	4. Does it have a happy ending and lead into the future?	_____
	5. Does it advocate a good cause that ignites and unites? Will listeners spread the word to the world about your brand?	_____
STRATEGIC	1. Is it structured (e.g. a vertical take-off, intro, middle, end)?	_____
	2. Does it have key elements (e.g. a heroine/hero, call to adventure, journey, strategic choices, guardians of the threshold, crossing the threshold, dilemmas, turning points, magical flights, resolution, etc.)?	_____
	3. Does it have inherent drama?	_____
	4. Does it shape how listeners see you? Is it visionary?	_____
	5. Is it told through performance?	_____

Repeat the signature story

Using the 5 cornerstones and the 25 defining characteristics, craft your signature story now. Next, tell it afresh (Figure E2.2).

Seeing is doing

Good things start with sensory imagination. Exercise visualization to maintain a positive self-image and corporate identity – and to bring about the success of the change initiative.

Individually, choose a place to sit where you feel others will not disturb you easily. Shut your eyes, sit in silence for a few minutes and take a few deep

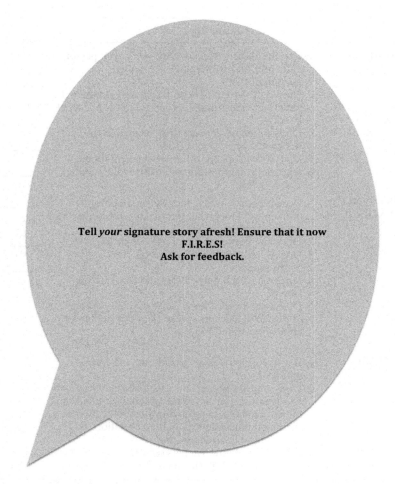

Figure E2.2 F.I.R.E.S.

breaths to unwind. Take your time to do this. Listen to a text with your mind's eye open. Imagine that you are experiencing this change situation right now. Zoom in on the imagery. Allow your imagination to create the situation described in the passage as vividly as possible. Concentrate on the voices/sounds you can hear and the images you can see, as well as the feelings you access.

1 The script

Positive beliefs can enormously help achieve desired outcomes. Visualize yourself as a recognized expert who has an important mission to embark on and who has a significant effect on a lot of people, day after day. You love what you do with all your heart and you're perfectly fit for change. Picture yourself striding confidentially into your office. You greet others cheerily.

You know your super-powers well. You're a positive leader. You're dressed smartly, beaming radiantly, and highly energized. Your positive energy is contagious. Imagine yourself building and sustaining high-quality connections with your work colleagues and passionately launching into the change initiative. Everyone greets your imaginative ideas and contribution warmly. Now, work energetically toward the intended outcome. See yourself truly happy and excited and satisfied – the condition you'll experience when this ultimate change purpose has been ticked off. You can do well if you bring your strengths to it. Yes, you can accomplish "moonshots"!

Now, to re-experience it in your mind, read the script over silently. Next, read it out loud, changing the text from second person to first person singular as you read. Remember, you are the one!

2 Energizing verbs and doodling

After you are back from your "guided trip," cover your table with a paper tablecloth, grab colored pens and crayons, and doodle your stories, thoughts, emotions, and information (Figure E2.3) and free your artistic expression!

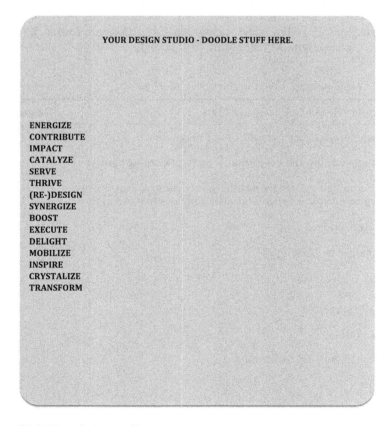

Figure E2.3 Your design studio

To stimulate ideas about how the initiative can be implemented successfully, identify ways in which the intended change outcomes can be achieved. To aid this, use a list of 15 of the most energizing verbs in English from Figure E2.3.

3 Share

Share your graffiti with others, and have collaborative change conversations.

Alternatively, limit the doodling to pictures only. Be free! Do it the way you want, color it the way you want. Be Picasso! Be Banksy! Be Van Gogh (but keep your ears intact …)!

Big 4 leadership ways: self-assessment inventory

What kind of a leader are you?

Fourfold leadership design is made up of Big 4 leadership ways: (1) thinking energizer (TE); (2) people organizer (PO); (3) strategic navigator (SN); and (4) innovator-designer (ID). Each leadership way has 13 "super-powers." After you have rated each of the items, go to the "Fourfold leadership design" and give yourself an overall rating (High, Medium, or Low). Then decide which strengths need boosting and, finally, note an Action Plan for yourself.

Instructions: For each "super-power" in Table E3.1, rate your own strength by marking H (High), M (Medium), or L (Low).

Table E3.1 Leadership way: thinking energizer (TE)

Leadership way: thinking energizer (TE)	Rating
Self-awareness, self-understanding, self-regulation	
A constant learning and development crafter (learning agility)	
A positive energizer (energizing others; modeling positive energy; managing energy; creating and sustaining positive energy)	
Physically energized	
Emotionally energized	
Mentally energized	
Spiritually energized	
Positive thinking	
Professional and positive identity	
Charisma	

Leadership way: thinking energizer (TE)	*Rating*
Honesty/ethics; value-focused; having the courage to say "no" to activity that is harmful to society at large	
Personal humility; staying grounded	
Resiliency (willing to jump in and get things started)	

Instructions: For each "super-power" in Table E3.2, rate your own strength by marking H (High), M (Medium), or L (Low).

Table E3.2 Leadership way: people operator (PO)

Leadership way: people operator (PO)	*Rating*
People skills (team member, motivating, recognizing others, celebrating team wins...)	
Positive communication skills	
Active listening skills	
Coaching skills	
A talent designer and developer	
Empathy and deep human understanding	
Socializing	
A networker (building positive energy networks and positive relationships)	
An employee and culture champion and evangelist	
Providing opportunities for people to receive/develop best self-feedback/portraits	
Diversity and cross-cultural sensitivity	
Positive influence skills	
A philanthropist: whether local, regional, national, or global (e.g., supplying jobs, supporting schools, nurturing start-ups); service/ servant leadership (e.g., volunteering)	

Instructions: For each "super-power" in Table E3.3, rate your own strength by marking H (High), M (Medium), or L (Low).

Table E3.3 Leadership way: strategic navigator (SN)

Leadership way: strategic navigator (SN)	Rating
Strategizing to win	
Optimizing the present, unlearning the past, inventing a new business model	
Being stakeholder-focused; navigating competition strategically	
Leading positive change by energizing, redesigning, and gelling	
Developing political and organizational agility; managing resistance	
Super-flexibility	
Assessing risks	
Proactivity (an inclination to respond purposefully to events)	
Project leadership	
Anti-bureaucracy	
Scenario crafting; being forward-looking	
Openness to new ideas	
Speed (thinking fast, deciding fast, sustaining speed)	

Instructions: For each "super-power" in Table E3.4, rate your own strength by marking H (High), M (Medium), or L (Low).

Table E3.4 Leadership way: innovator-designer (ID)

Leadership way: innovator-designer (ID)	Rating
Super-creativity	
Pioneering, innovative, imaginative	
Focusing on the big picture (moonshots, actualizing vision, strategic intent)	
A conceptualizer (visual: awakening, exploration, strategy and communication); storyteller (using business narrative to transform the organization)	
Design thinking skills (*What already is? What if anything were possible? What wows? What works?*)	
An initiative planner and executor	
A problem-solver (identifying enablers)	

Leadership way: innovator-designer (ID)	*Rating*
A customer-driven co-creator (experience design and mapping)	
Positive resource utilization and lean thinking	
Prompting high levels of project and organization performance	
An evidence-based architect (total quality mindset, profitability)	
Innovation transfer (including know-how assets transfer)	
Being tech-smart	

Fourfold leadership design self-portrait

Now check your Big 4 scores in Table E3.5.

Table E3.5 Guide to Big 4 scores

Rating	Quality	Description
H	:-)	Very good leadership qualities
M	:-|	Leadership qualities need improvement
L	:-(	Leadership qualities deficits

Leadership strengths

In Table E3.6 rate your strengths.

Table E3.6 What are your strengths? What needs boosting?

Rating	:-)	:-|	:-(
	H	M	L
Thinking energizer			
Your rating			
People operator			
Your rating			
Strategic navigator			
Your rating			
Innovator-designer			
Your rating			

Action plan

1. How do you feel about the way you lead? Does anything about your leadership portrait surprise you? Which aspects of your leadership profile are the most thought-provoking to you? What energizes you?

_____

_____

_____

2. How does the way you lead affect you? How does the way you lead affect your team? How does the way you lead affect your organization? How does the way you lead affect your industry?

_____

_____

_____

3. List four baby steps you could take during your next working week to boost your leadership qualities and super-powers. What about the next three months? Six months? Who will hold you accountable for your actions (your family, friends, work group, line manager, HR team)? What resources will you need?

_____

_____

_____

4. What are some of the things that may be blocking your way and hindering your progress as a leader? Can you dream up new strategies that might help you to overcome these major blocks to your positive leadership presence, and to accomplish "moonshots"?

_____

_____

_____

Continuing self-coaching: becoming a corporate Olympian

First, complete the self-assessment questionnaire and then outline the baby steps and expectations for self-development based on your strengths.

Complete the self-assessment questionnaire in Table E3.7 – and make doing so a routine!

Table E3.7 Continuing self-coaching: becoming a corporate Olympian

	Self-development check-in	Not true of me	Slightly true of me	Quite a bit true of me	Definitely true of me	Very true of me
Role	*Today/this week I brought my A game to:*	1	2	3	4	5
TE	energize my workplace/home					
	develop some skill(s) or learn something new					
	choose and show my positive leadership presence					
	Total for Thinking Energizer (TE)					
	Priority for Thinking Energizer (High, Medium, Low)					
PO	do someone a favor/service					
	recognize other people's talent					
	authentically listen, demonstrate empathy and deep human understanding					
	Total for People Operator (PO)					
	Priority for People Operator (High, Medium, Low)					
SN	exercise agility					
	have winning aspirations and strategize to win					
	lead change positively					
	Total for Strategic Navigator (SN)					
	Priority for Strategic Navigator (High, Medium, Low)					
ID	employ imagination					
	design something new					
	combat some "wicked" problem experimentally					
	Total for Innovator-Designer (ID)					
	Priority for Innovator-Designer (High, Medium, Low)					

Set baby steps and expectations for self-development based on your strengths in Table E3.8.

Table E3.8 Baby steps and expectations for self-development based on your strengths

Roles	Total scores (0 = min; 15 = max)	Priority rankings (H = 3, M = 2, L = 1)	Baby steps and expectations (specify target dates and success metrics)
Thinking energizer (TE)			
People operator (PO)			
Strategic navigator (SN)			
Innovator-designer (ID)			

Guide to scores
0–6 Qualities deficits – this is an evident and immediate developmental need for you.
7–11 This may well be a developmental need for you, depending on your priorities.
12–15 You seem well developed in this role at this time. You may still wish to develop further this strength in yourself.
These scores indicate your situation now. This can change at any time.

Positive workplace culture fit

1. Integrate the 3Ss. A positive and energizing workplace culture can only exist by integrating the three *S*s (A. *Selection* of "positive energizers," B. positive *Socialization* and development, and C. *System* of recognition and rewards) in a positive workplace culture triangle (PWCT) (Figure E4.1). How does yours stack up?
2. Select and engage "positive energizers." Add in more qualities in Table E4.1.
3. Review and exercise initiative-specific staff "strengths" (= abilities to provide reliable, near-perfect performance in a given activity) in Table E4.2.

Positive workplace cultural assets audit (PWCA-20)

What is best about your workplace? Determine how you feel about your work environment. Assess where your enterprise stands today on the 20 cultural assets, responding "V" (*Like my organization*), "X" (*Somewhat*), or "–" (*Unlike my organization*) in Table E5.1.

B. Positive Socialization and Development

POSITIVE
WORKPLACE
CULTURE
TRIANGLE

A. Selection of "Positive Energizers"   C. System of Recognition and Rewards

Figure E4.1 Positive workplace culture triangle

Table E4.1 Energized quality

Energized employees	Not energized employees	De-energized employees
Energize the workplace	Put their time, but not energy/strengths, into their work	De-energize the workplace
High performing	Not high performing	Busy indulging in their de-energized behavior
Boost others	Not interested in others	Diminish others
Optimistic	Not confident	Critical
Flexible	Sleepwalking through their workday	Inflexible
Honoring	Not charitable	Selfish
Moral	Amoral	Immoral
…	…	…
…	…	…
…	…	…

Table E4.2 Initiative-specific strengths review

Initiative-specific strengths review			
Identification and selection	*Focused interview questions (Describe a time when you ...)*	*Role-playing scenarios*	*Past work history*
Talents (Their natural selves/ ways of thinking, feeling, and behaving – gained naturally)			
Skills (Basic abilities to carry out important tasks – gained via practice and training)			
Knowledge (Understanding of facts – gained via experience and education)			
Attitude (A settled way of thinking or feeling about someone/something, typically one that is reflected in a person's behavior)			

Table E5.1 Positive workplace cultural assets audit (PWCA-20)

Cultural assets	I feel that...	Response
1. Visionary leadership and foresight	We're carrying out tomorrow's business well today	
2. Positive organizational climate and entrepreneurial energy	We're a genuine hot-spot, buzzing with positive energy and open innovation. The workforce's energized and people can truly thrive here	
3. Employee voice and co-determination	We find ourselves empowered to organize ourselves into small and supportive teams, and operate with minimal supervision. We can appoint our own leaders and work out for ourselves how to respond to challenges	
4. A clear purpose and meaning	We believe that ... because ... Therefore, we exist to ...	
5. Stories, symbols, and rituals	The hero/founder story's told as a form of oral history to spread, shape, and cement our culture and identity	

Cultural assets	I feel that...	Response
6. A winning strategy	We have a detailed organizational roadmap for the intended change outcomes. Our organization-wide and functional policies, philosophies and practices are strategically well aligned	
7. Evidence-based management (e.g., HRM, reward system)	Decision-making is built upon research-based evidence	
8. Positive relationship network	The quality of connections between employees is high; people cultivate trust, compassion, servant leadership, diversity, and recognition in this place	
9. Flexibility and work-life integration	We choose to work here because our organization is a family-friendly one; we can work from home when we need to	
10. Agility and change leadership practices	We're a nimble enterprise, good at leading positive change in a methodological as well as a creative way	
11. Constant learning & development (L&D)	We thrive on action and social learning in this spot, exploiting learning through (reverse) mentoring for development, coaching, and building high-quality connections and networks	
12. An external and internal focus	Both increased engagement with external actors, and increased collaboration and internal integration come into play	
13. Digital presence	We're present on popular social media	
14. Reputation	We've managed to build brand energy and recognition, and instill consumers' trust and loyalty	
15. An ethical code	We're guided by a compass of ethics and we do the right thing	
16. Customer-driven excellence	The consumer is boss here	
17. A horizon-scanning capability and R&D skills	We're an expert horizon scanner: we keep a sharp lookout for the "next big thing"	
18. Creativity	We're a design-thinking and design-driven company – we like to think like designers do, which means going beyond "beautiful" as well as going beyond "analytics"	
19. Continuous process and quality improvement	We've successfully deployed lean thinking	
20. Play	Work's as much fun as play here	

Guide to scores
Give 3 points for V
Give 2 points for X;
Give 1 point for —
Workplace culture: 0–20 Negative; 21–32 Deficient; 33–47 Neutral; 48–60 Positive.

Fun@work

Fun is an experience that can be purposeful. Apply the strategies of three kinds of fun to boost it in the workplace (Figure E5.1)!

Using Table E5.2, make your change initiative more fun!

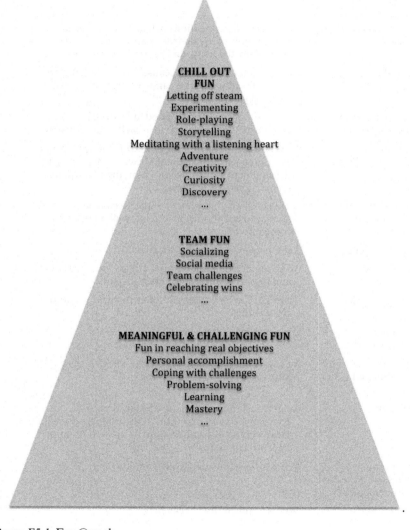

Figure E5.1 Fun@work

Table E5.2 Making your change initiative more fun

Change initiative as	*List activities that can provide exciting opportunities of playing and having fun*
1. Energizer	Booster shot workshops Pure fun activities Physical energizers Mental aerobics …
2. Storytelling	Crafting the story Visiting the future followed by planning Deploying an energizing vision …
3. Test	Running disciplined experiments Routine revisions to plans …
4. Fellowship	Corporate retreats …
5. Going deeper	Imaginative contemplation exercises …
6. Discovery	Awakening …

5   The Redesign WorkBox
10 tools

The Redesign WorkBox contents

Redesign

ToolBox	Dynamic actions	Tools, worksheets and exercises		
REDESIGN WorkBox	**R1.** Co-craft the "sunnier side of life" in strategic collaboration with organizational members and stakeholders, by way of collective design thinking and appreciative future search (*What is already working well? What if anything were possible? What exactly wows? What happens to that, if we do this?*)	Sunnier Side of Life Search	Picture It!	I.M.A.G.I.N.E.R. Innovation Booster
	R2. Remodel organizational structure, processes, and components, if necessary	Optimizer		
	R3. Navigate and manage power and politics, resistance, a change coalition (e.g., a dedicated "design team") and core business	Strategic Stakeholder Ecosystem Navigator	Quick and Positive Comebacks	
	R4. Coach and develop for positive leadership, engagement, and organizational renewal	Coach's Self-Check	Coaching Conversations To G.R.O.W.	
	R5. Before roll-out, run disciplined learning launches to de-risk change initiative execution	Disciplined Learning Launches		

Sunnier side of life search

Want to find your way to a better future? Here's how. Master "future search" protocol components, questions, and interventions. Add more items to Table R1.1. Then lead a collective sunnier side of life search summit to visit the future.

Lead a collective sunnier side of life search summit to visit the future, using the protocol in Table R1.2.

Picture it!

Application of cognitive frame semantics to organizational analysis

It's always good to get feedback from the employees of any establishment. After all, they are the ones who make the change and they are the ones who

Table R1.1 Sunnier side of life search

Appreciative inquiry components	Draft search questions	Example interventions
Positive performance inquiry (discovery)	*What is already working well?*	Change scorecard Organization fitness audit Value chain analysis Organizational and environmental scanning Employee strengths profiling
Positive distance inquiry: source-path-goal schema (dream)	*What if anything were possible?*	Envisioning possibilities Journey mapping Working towards "Everest goals" and "moonshots"
Positive intervention selection (design)	*What wows?*	Design sprints and co-creating Total reward management Performance appraisals Job analysis and aids Work (re-)design interventions Work-life integration Positive feedback Knowledge management Tech transfer Constant learning and development Learning contracts
Positive execution (deployment)	*What happens to that, if we do this?*	Disciplined learning launches Process consultation Coaching and mentoring Positive communication Storytelling Evaluation, monitoring, learning, *re*learning and *un*learning *Open* innovation

Table R1.2 An example: a fictional consulting boutique

Future search protocol
Affirmative theme: How could we jointly build and sustain high-quality connections in the workplace, and develop energized teams of consultants for future success?

Appreciate what works well	• What energizes you? What gives life to your team and organization? • Without being humble, share some high-point time you experienced while working here when the case you needed to deal with made you feel proud. What was going on? Who did you connect with? • Tell a story of a time when you enjoyed some peak experience as a team member – something that energized you lots, and caused a glow of personal/team satisfaction, a moment when you really, really wanted to work here. Why did you feel this way? What made this fantastic cooperation possible? • What exactly do we do well?
Envision an attainable new future and results	• Imagine it's 2030, and you are awarded the Top Partner by the CEO for developing a firm that stands for the best professionals. What do others notice about you and your team? How did you play a part in achieving this big dream? • What are the key features of some five forces that may shape the team's future? You can pick anything you like.
Co-create what should be the ideal	• At X, we respect others greatly. This begins with our junior associates. • We're consultants who carry out our daily professional duties in a professional way. • To us, it's virtuous to encourage each other. It's honorable to serve our clients. • We're proud to be X because ... • We continually learn as we work.
Sustain the sunnier side of life	• How can we execute the dreamed design best? Here are these great scenarios... What do you think? • Who is going to do what and by when? • What action steps will we take right now (today/tomorrow/ next week/next month) to accomplish our big dream? What milestones, measures, and metrics can we implement to accelerate progress toward our Everest goal(s) and moonshots?

---

are most affected by it. One way of engaging everyone in change, or even seeing how the change is going to be shaped, is to get them to "picture" it.

Ask employees to describe the enterprise and how it now functions by "picturing it" to generate mental images in the form of analogies, metaphors, or similes for the present situation (Table R1.3). Analyze the images and symbols. All the proffered images and symbols should be thoroughly analyzed as this gives a true picture of what is now, and how what will be is perceived.

Then, review the organization's position by asking three fundamental questions on the position of the organization in the employees' view and act immediately to fix the gap between the pictured and target organization.

Review the organization's position by asking the employees three fundamental questions (Table R1.4).

Act immediately to close the gap for between H-Agreement items, using Table R1.5. For L-Agreement items, make sure you first arrive at a consensus over Q1 and Q2 above, at the minimum.

Table R1.3 Picture it!

"What-is" mental image	*Analysis of "what-is"*
Our organization is like a well-oiled machine.	It operates well.
We're busy bees.	We're energetic, diligent, and hard-working.
Our business is a dinosaur.	It's unresponsive to change, and moving toward extinction.
The owners are making us work like dogs.	They're making us work extremely hard.
We're rich in ideas.	Ideas are money.
We're climbing the industry ladder.	Our status is going up.
Although we're an established enterprise, we like to think in terms of "moonshots."	We think in terms of achieving breakthrough innovation, believing that a "moonshot" is a path toward renewed leadership under radically new tech and cultural conditions.
...	...
...	...
...	...

Table R1.4 Review the organization's position by asking strategic questions

Strategic questions	*Organization's position*	*Agreement: H (High)/L (Low)*
Q1. Where are we now, and why?		H/L
Q2. If anything were possible, where do we want to be?		H/L
Q3. How do we get there?		H/L

Table R1.5 The gap and the immediate action to close the gap

Gap	Immediate action to close the gap
...	Boost/enhance/concentrate more on ...
...	Dig deeper to revise the defined objective(s)
...	Manage organizational complexity by ...
...	Design/develop/deliver interventions for...
...	Roadmap/re-design ...
...	...

I.M.A.G.I.N.E.R.

"What if ...?" "Suppose we do this?" "What would have to be true?" – these are key questions in building positive strategic change.

Use the I.M.A.G.I.N.E.R prompts to generate exciting ideas for (new) products and services. You can also add more questions. Then use the Innovation Booster Matrix (IBM) in Table R1.6 to develop energizing questions and (re-)design concepts. Finally, recognize how benefits, needs, feelings, and actions interrelate to unlock new potential.

Integrate
Maximize
Adjust
Google
Interchange
Negate/Knock out
Exchange
Re-energize

Integrate

- What if we integrated X with something else?
- What might we mix to make it more attractive, more functional, and more human-centered?
- How could we integrate its design with strategic decisions in operations (quality, process, inventory, capacity)?
- What would happen if, when designing it, we engaged with (extreme) users and integrated various functional areas to cooperate and work together in the same time frame?

Your question(s):

Maximize

- How could we make the best use of it?
- What would happen if we made it as large or great as possible?
- How might we boost its value ratio (usefulness/quality to cost), the value stream of the process for the product/service (steps and tasks executed to complete a product or deliver a service from beginning to end) as well as maximize growth opportunities?
- What attribute(s) of it could we magnify to produce something new?

Your question(s):

_____

_____

Adjust

- How could we restyle the makeup, look, feel of it?
- What if we depended on economies of scope (a high variety of products from a single process) and were able to provide customized products at approximately same costs as mass production?
- How might we be more flexible and adjust it to new conditions?
- Could we convert it into something (totally) else?

Your question(s):

_____

_____

Google

- What if we Googled it for ideas?
- What if we used Google Images?
- What if we used Google Videos?
- What if we used Google News?

Your question(s):

_____

_____

Interchange

- What if we did the exact opposite of what we're trying to do right now?
- Could we reverse roles?
- What if we rearranged things?
- Could we interchange components/protocols?

Your question(s):

_____

_____

Negate/Knock out

- How could we simplify it/the process?
- What if it were smaller, lighter, more focused?
- What would happen if we eliminated complexity and costs associated with large number of unnecessary variations?
- What if, to eliminate waste (non-value-added activities) or subtracting the frills, we deployed lean thinking and removed some components (could less become more?)?

Your questions(s):

_____

_____

Exchange

- What if we used it as a substitute for something else?
- What other products/processes could we use in place of it?
- What would happen if we replaced materials/resources?
- If we couldn't fail, what options would we have then?

Your question(s):

_____

_____

Re-energize

- What would happen if we revitalized it?
- How could we re-design/remodel its physical features, technical requirements and/or production process so that someone else could use it?
- How could we reprocess it to use it again in another context?
- How could we recycle the waste from it to create something new?

Your question(s):

_____

_____

Innovation booster

The only way that positive change will come is if we are energized to create and sustain the change. The only way to unlock potential and be innovative is to ask the right questions and use the right tools. The Innovation Booster is the right tool.

Use the Innovation Booster Matrix (IBM) in Table R1.6 to develop energizing questions and (re-)design concepts.

Table R1.6 Innovation booster

Benefits	Needs	Positive feelings	Action
Access	Acceptance	Affectionate	Add
Autonomy	Affection	Appreciative	Adjust
Assurance	Appreciation	Blissful	Analyze
Awareness	Authenticity	Comfortable	Boost
Choice	Autonomy	Compassionate	Convert
Co-creation	Beauty	Confident	Cooperate
Competence	Belonging	Curious	Create
Coolness	Challenge	Delighted	Customize
Delivery	Choice	Eager	Deploy
Design	Closeness	Empowered	Eliminate
Distribution	Communication	Encouraged	Engage
Durability	Connection	Energized	Exchange
Ease of use	Cooperation	Engaged	Execute
Education/Info	Creativity	Enlivened	Extend
Energy	Empathy	Excited	Google
Efficiency	Equality	Exhilarated	Improve
Flexibility	Freedom	Expectant	Inform
Fun	Harmony	Fascinated	Integrate
Functionality	Honesty	Friendly	Interchange
Innovation	Humor	Grateful	Knock out
Intangibles	Integrity	Happy	Lead
Luxury	Joy	Hopeful	Magnify
Online	Learning	Inspired	Manage
Packaging	Love	Involved	Maximize
Performance	Meaning	Joyful	Mix
Power	Participation	Loving	Operate
Price	Peace	Mellow	Outsource
Privacy	Physical well-being	Moved	Partner
Problem-solver	Play	Open	Provide
Quality	Presence	Optimistic	Re-arrange
Reliability	Purpose	Passionate	Redesign
Re-use	Respect	Peaceful	Re-energize
Speed	Security	Pleased	Restyle
Relatedness	Space	Refreshed	Recycle
Service Recovery/	Stability	Rejuvenated	Remodel
Guarantee			
Status	To be known	Renewed	Replace
Size	To be seen	Safe	Reprocess
Tangibles	To be understood	Satisfied	Revitalize
Uniqueness	Trust	Thrilled	Standardize
Vitality/Health	Warmth	Touched	Subtract

Using the Innovation Booster Matrix, recognize how benefits, needs, feelings, and actions interrelate to unlock new potential.

Combine benefits

- How could we emphasize its uniqueness by speed?
- How could we gain more access by increasing distribution networks?
- How could we increase/reduce size by going online?

New potential

_____

_____

Combine benefits with needs

- How could we make it more tangible so that they may appreciate it more?
- How could we offer better assurance so that we're the strategic advisor of choice to them, and more authentic, too?
- How could we be more flexible so that they stay connected?

New potential

_____

_____

Combine benefits with needs and feelings

- What could we do to energize the employees more so that they're more excited and more creative?
- How could we develop environmental awareness to restore integrity and confidence?
- How could we better protect their privacy so that they feel more comfortable and connected?

New potential

_____

_____

Select an action and insert it into the benefits/needs/feelings question

- What open innovation initiatives could we execute to encourage cooperation and re-use?

- Which business processes could we outsource to offer better service so that all are more satisfied?
- How could we revitalize design so that it is more purposeful and open?

New potential

_____

_____

Optimizer (O-10)

Re-modeling 10 critical components of organization design to lead positive organizational change and optimal performance

Scan your current organization design. Are all of the critical components of organization design in alignment? Indicate where you think they are on the 0–10 scale now (0 = misaligned; 10 = aligned). Give examples to support your position (survival/(sub)optimal/thriving). Next, on the same continuum, replicate it for the desired state (DS) as well as record actions to re-model/optimize components. Be aware that this is not a survey, but a consciousness-raising and discussion instrument on organizational alignment and optimal performance.

> (0) MISALIGNMENT-------MINIMAL PERFORMANCE
> (10) ALIGNMENT-----------OPTIMAL PERFORMANCE

1. Change purpose/strategy/competitive advantage NOW *(Example(s) to support your position):*

_____

Action item(s) for DS:

_____

2. Structure NOW *(Example(s) to support your position):*

_____

Action item(s) for DS:

_____

3. Skills NOW *(Example(s) to support your position):*

_____

Action item(s) for DS:

_____

4. Processes and lateral capability NOW *(Example(s) to support your position):*

_____

Action item(s) for DS:

_____

5. Incentives NOW *(Example(s) to support your position):*

_____

Action item(s) for DS:

_____

6. Pay system NOW *(Example(s) to support your position):*

_____

Action item(s) for DS:

_____

7. Resources NOW *(Example(s) to support your position):*

_____

Action item(s) for DS:

_____

8. People practices NOW *(Example(s) to support your position):*

Action item(s) for DS:

9. (Positive) Energy NOW *(Example(s) to support your position):*

Action item(s) for DS:

10. Action plan NOW *(Example(s) to support your position):*

Action item(s) for DS:

Relating to the organization design process, think holistically. Be cognizant of how alignment of all of the components of organization design produces optimal performance. Misalignment of any of the components of organization design will produce suboptimal performance. Match the components of organization design to the performance scenarios in Table R2.1.

In Table R2.2, address the misalignment/suboptimal performance scenarios. A corrective action deals with a misalignment/suboptimal performance that has occurred. A preventive action addresses the potential for a misalignment/suboptimal performance to occur.

Strategic stakeholder ecosystem navigator

Identify stakeholders

Some people have an interest in a company's or organization's affairs – they are called a stakeholder. To make sure positive change is a success, the support of stakeholders is necessary. If you follow this guide, your job as change leader will be much easier.

Table R2.1 Optimizer

Change purpose/ strategy/ competitive advantage	Structure (power and authority, reporting relationships, organizational roles)	Skills	Processes and lateral capability (networks, processes, teams, integrative roles)	Incentives	Pay system	Resources	People practices	Positive energy	Action plan	Performance scenario
										Optimal performance/ positive change
▓										Confusion
	▓									Friction
		▓								Anxiety
			▓							Gridlock
				▓						Sporadic change
					▓					Internal competition
						▓				Frustration
							▓			Low performance
								▓		Inactivity/ Negativity
									▓	False start

Table R2.2 Issues and action items

Issue	Enter corrective action items (reactive and immediate)	Enter preventive action items (proactive and strategic)
1. Confusion		
2. Friction		
3. Anxiety		
4. Gridlock		
5. Sporadic change		
6. Internal competition		
7. Frustration		
8. Low performance		
9. Inactivity/ Negativity		
10. False start		

Table R3.1 Strategic stakeholder ecosystem navigator

Stakeholders interested in the issue

Internal	Stake	Power source	External	Stake	Power source
Staff			Customers		
Unions			Suppliers		
Contractors			Community		
...			...		
...			...		
...			...		

Identify the key stakeholders interested in the issue to prevent important ones being left out, using Table R3.1. This tool will be critical in managing stakeholders throughout the project life-cycle.

Categorize clients

Now categorize your clients into *those who know* (= aware of the issue), *those who care* (= may suffer from it), and *those who can* (= the sponsors – they have the authority to give the green light for the project) (Figure R3.1). Map out stakeholders on the power-stake priority dynamics grid (Table R3.2). Answer the following strategic questions with Yes (Y), No (N), or Not Applicable (N/A) in Table R3.3. Next, create an action plan and proactively

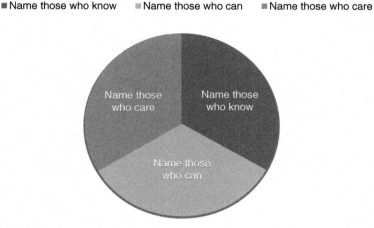

Figure R3.1 Client categories

Table R3.2 Power-stake priority dynamics grid

P O W E R	High	**Keep satisfied**	**Manage closely**
	Low	**Monitor**	**Keep informed**
		Low	High
		STAKE	

consult and engage key stakeholders to better manage risk and navigate the process toward an intended change outcome.

Quick and positive comebacks

Left to themselves, humans will naturally commit to half a change rather than going the whole hog. This never works, so confidence must be restored, and change will again march forth to battle. Follow this guide to positively influence dissenters and get change done!

Practice and think up creative replies to the statements of resistance. There's space for this in Table R3.4.

Table R3.3 Strategic question and action item

Strategic question	Check box	Action item
Can we meet the concerns/build and sustain high-quality relationships critical for initiative success?	…	
Can we boost the power/stake of the current stakeholders who are pro the project?	…	
Can we minimize the power/stake of the antagonists?	…	
Can we engage new stakeholders to shift the balance/politics?	…	
Can the hostility/resistance torpedo the initiative? If yes, can we somehow re-energize the proposal to break it?	…	

Table R3.4 Quick and positive comebacks

Lines of resistance to change	Possible quick and positive comebacks
I've never been so scared. Will this work at all?	*I understand you may not feel 100% comfortable with the change, which is only natural. In fact, brain science research shows that change taps fear receptors in the brain and taxes the brain's cognitive capacity to learn new ways of doing things. Change is often messy for sure but we've planned it well and therefore we're quite ready for it. If we pull together and implement it, we'll all be better off.*
Your alternative response:	
But I don't want to.	*For what reason? What concerns you most right now? Please help me understand how you see this.*
Your alternative response:	
I'm feeling so tired.	*So you're overloaded and feeling under the weather. Sounds like you're having a tough time today. OK, if you could do anything you wanted to feel more energized, what exactly would you do? What pointers would you give someone else who's dealing with the same challenge?*
Your alternative response:	

(Continued)

Lines of resistance to change	Possible quick and positive comebacks
I think it's a mad idea. I am NOT doing it. Period. Your alternative response:	*Why don't you think it over and get back to me later on today? OR: It seems we're at an impasse. I'm not prepared to agree but I wouldn't like to walk away either. Perhaps we should spend some time looking into our respective objectives.*
I believe we're inadequately prepared. Your alternative response:	*What exactly do we have wrong/missing? Is there another way to explain this?*
We want X, Y, Z resources! We won't get going. Your alternative response:	*Why's that critical for you? OK, here's a possibility…*
I don't understand what you want me to do. Your alternative response:	*Please tell me specifically what you're not clear about concerning what you're being requested to do.*
But it's *always* worked this way in the past, so we know well how to advance it to the next level. We've done it before, so we can do it again. Your alternative response:	*Old ways were great in the past, yet they were designed for how things stood that now changed. So what can we do to lead a renaissance while capitalizing on tradition?*
We'd better launch it in X department first. Your alternative response:	*Thanks! I'm grateful for your advice with respect to X, and we'll be taking care of X, too. Now, what I'd like you to particularly focus on is…*
So, you're pressing me to do this? Your alternative response:	*I'm so sorry you may consider it a difficulty but we've mulled it over and it's critical now for us that the intended change initiative outcomes get achieved. Let's try, OK?*

Lines of resistance to change	Possible quick and positive comebacks
Z (=*someone senior*) isn't gonna think well of this change.	*Well, I've already consulted Z. Z's been involved and is on the side of the change initiative. But, now, how else could you be of service?*
Your alternative response:	
If we don't get A, we won't do X. If we don't get B, we won't do Y, either. If we don't get C, we won't be doing Z ...	*If you're not ready to work with me toward a mutually sustainable outcome, I can't afford to spend more time talking.*
Your alternative response:	
We'll be working on this next week.	*The situation's actually quite urgent. By the way, is there anything extremely serious that makes you unable to start this week?*
Your alternative response:	
Awesome! We're loving this! (= *ironic tone*)	*I'm so pleased that you're liking it so much! I'm sure your energy and enthusiasm will be tremendous assets to the proposed change. Now, who's exactly doing what exactly by when exactly?*
Your alternative response:	
You owe me one.	*Yes, I'll keep in mind that I owe you one. Yet, it's high time we got down to some serious work now.*
Your alternative response:	

Coaching and coach's self-check: helping extremely good leaders to further succeed

In the past, if you told someone you were a coach, their response would likely have been, "Wow! What sport?" Today, organizational coaching is one of the fastest-growing professions in the world. Let's consider different *helping* roles first in Table R4.1. Then we'll discuss the necessary attitudes, behaviors, and competences that a good coach needs in Table R4.2, followed by a look at positive coaching design. The leader/coach should do a self-assessment in Table R4.3 and, finally, produce a coaching growth plan.

Table R4.1 Helping: different roles

Attitudes, behaviors and competencies (ABCs) of different helping roles					
Therapist	*Consultant*	*Manager*	*Trainer*	*Mentor*	*Teacher*
Goes back, diagnoses and "fixes" dysfunctionality	Analyzes; gives recommendations and roadmaps; Influences but has no direct power	Manages and has direct responsibility	Identifies skills gaps and trains	Creates and sustains a partnership that helps mentees to continuously learn and develop	Tests, teaches, tests
Log more attitudes, behaviors and competencies (ABCs)					
...	...	...	...	...	...
...	...	...	...	...	...

Helping: different roles

Coach's ABCs

Table R4.2 Coach's attitudes, behaviors, and competencies (ABCs)

Coach	*Log more of the coach's ABCs*
Looks forward and helps clients develop themselves and achieve their personal and professional best; energizes, asks penetrating questions and listens deeply	

Positive coaching design

Building and sustaining high-quality connections between the coach and the coachee is necessary (Figure R4.1).

Five fundamental principles of extremely good coaching (FP-5)

FP1 The client sets the agenda.

FP2 The client is resourceful and has huge potential.

FP3 The coach uses clear evidence-based methodology but doesn't deliver answers. The coach energizes, asks, listens, and invites the client to discover, dream, redesign, and deliver.

FP4 The coach helps extremely good leaders further succeed.

FP5 The coach-client relationship is a synergistic, professional, and equal one.

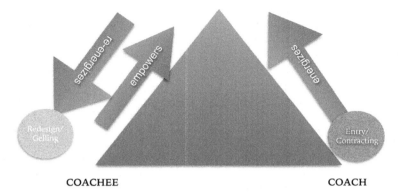

POSITIVE COACHING RELATIONSHIP

COACHEE   COACH

Figure R4.1 Positive coaching relationship

The coach's self-check (CSC-50)

For each of the 50 coaching competency areas in Table R4.3, rate your strength level by marking H (High), M (Medium), L (Low), or N (Nonexistent).

Table R4.3 Coach's self-check

Coach's attitudes, behaviors and competencies (ABCs)	Rating
1. Entry and contracting	
2. Building high-quality connections	
3. Setting ground rules and the stage	
4. Managing expectations	
5. Setting specific performance goals	
6. Being authentic	
7. Cultural and emotional intelligence quotient	
8. Structuring and using clear research-based methodologies, tools, and techniques	
9. Checking in	
10. Energizing and empowering	

(Continued)

Coach's attitudes, behaviors and competencies (ABCs)	Rating

11. Challenging

12. Focusing

13. Physical expressiveness

14. Power of speech

15. Self-awareness

16. Eye contact

17. Spontaneity, intuition, and humor

18. Positive leadership presence

19. Tracking

20. Monitoring progress

21. Rewarding improvement and acknowledging

22. Serving as a sounding board

23. Dialogue and discovery skills

24. Asking powerful, curious, and thought-provoking questions

25. Active and reflective listening with empathy and without judgment

26. Listening to dig deeper

27. Playing back what you heard

28. Filtering, clarifying, and reframing

29. Thought-showering

30. Assumption testing

31. Visualization and metaphor

32. Evoking creativity and innovation

33. Paying attention to what is said

Coach's attitudes, behaviors and competencies (ABCs)	*Rating*

34. Giving timely, specific, and constructive feedback open-heartedly

35. Working with personal issues, conflicts, and failure

36. Nailing it down

37. Using silence resourcefully

38. Being open to outcome

39. Triggering reflection

40. Following through

41. Summarizing

42. Managing and coaching self

43. Managing time and energy

44. Expertise, constant learning, and development

45. Evaluating and measuring ROI

46. Active networking

47. Credibility and accountability

48. Passion and compassion

49. Trust and confidentiality

50. Code of Professional Conduct

TOTAL:

Number of Hs: _____ Number of Ms: _____ Number of Ls: _____ Number of Ns: _____

Guide to scores
Give 3 points for H
Give 2 points for M
Give 1 point for L
Give 0 for N
Total ranking: _____

LEVEL I (0–49) Has never delivered coaching/Does not use coaching
LEVEL II (50–74) Absolute beginner
LEVEL III (75–99) Gateway
LEVEL IV (100–124) Higher
LEVEL V (125–150) Pro

Coaching growth plan

Note down your ideas for a coaching growth plan.

1. Desired outcome(s):

2. Specific goal(s) and objective(s):

3. What specific competencies do you need to develop (*Boost Ms, Ls, and Ns*)?

4. What's holding you back?

5. What resources will you likely need?

6. Action steps:

7. Who will hold you accountable?

8. Define success criteria, target dates for check-ins and completion:

9. Evaluation:

10. Further notes:

Coaching Conversations To G.R.O.W: From Theme to Way Forward

To get results, to make positive change possible, you have to ask questions. The right questions, however, need be asked – this is a list of them.

Master these 150 penetrating questions. Use them when you hold your ongoing, one-on-one, face-to-face sessions with your team members/direct reports/subordinates (working session length: approx. 60–90 mins; frequency: preferably twice a month, depending on life-cycle rhythm of work). Keep the conversation cycle: *Theme–Goal–Real Life–Options and Obstacles–Way Forward*.

COACHING CONVERSATION STAGE: THEME

- What's on your mind?
- What would you like to talk about/concentrate on now?
- What would be the most essential topic of conversation to focus on today?
- Can you tell me about your day today?
- What did you accomplish since we last spoke?
- What's become clear since we last met?
- What's happened since we last spoke?
- What's new/the latest/the update?
- Where are you this day?
- What's the *real* challenge here for you?
- ***Your favorite question(s):*** ....

COACHING CONVERSATION STAGE: GOAL

- What do you want?
- What would you like to take away from this coaching session today?
- What would you like to achieve by the end of our conversation?
- What's the clear and specific goal you want to achieve?
- Why is the goal desirable for you?
- What's your desired outcome?
- What exactly do you want to achieve in the short/medium/long term?
- How can I help/best coach you in this situation?
- What would you like to occur?
- How critical is this for you now?
- What is your winning aspiration?
- How would you rate your achievements so far in this respect?
- Why's that so important to you?

- How will you know if you reach your goal?
- How could you break down the goal into more manageable sub-goals?
- What would be the best thing, the best outcome about fulfilling your wish, and how would fulfilling your wish make you feel?
- How will you measure it?
- ***Your favorite question(s):*** ....

COACHING CONVERSATION STAGE: <u>R</u>EAL LIFE

- What's your life *really* about?
- What's going on?
- What's *really* happening here?
- What's the big picture?
- What's the bigger picture?
- What energizes you?
- What does your perfect day look like?
- What should your life motto be?
- What's the biggest dream for yourself these days?
- What seems to be the problem/trouble here?
- What's bothering/eating you?
- What's (not) working?
- How does it look to you?
- Why haven't you reached this goal already?
- What does that mean for you?
- It seems that this is hard – can you just name it?
- What caused it?
- What led up to it?
- For life to be perfect, what should happen then?
- Who will be the winners and losers if you get what you want?
- What's out of harmony here, and how can we restore it?
- Is the life you're living now a result of your own choices or the choices of other people?
- What's the lie?
- Are you holding on to something you may need to let go perhaps?
- What do you want me to know about it?
- Can you tell me (more) about it?
- Can you give (more) evidence?
- What about the facts?
- How do you feel about it?
- What needs to change here?
- How I can be your hero coach today?

- Can you help me understand how you see the situation?
- What would be the best question to ask you right now to help you think clearly about this situation?
- What's your favorite way of sabotaging yourself and your "moonshot" goals?
- When in your life did you stop having big dreams/telling stories/having fun?
- If you won the lottery, what would you do then?
- Is there another way to explain this?
- Who/what/where/how much ...?
- Why (not)?
- What are you (un)willing to change?
- What conversations are you avoiding now?
- What do you mean?
- What's the lesson here?
- What do you think would perhaps be holding you back if you believed you could make your own luck?
- Do you pretend to know or not to know?
- What are you resisting?
- What's stopping you?
- What are you *not* telling me?
- Is there anything else (you remember)?
- Have you been here before?
- Who's in control here?
- What have you done about this up to now?
- ***Your favorite question(s):*** ....

COACHING CONVERSATION STAGE: <u>O</u>PTIONS and <u>O</u>BS-TACLES

- What options do you have?
- What else?
- If you're saying 'yes' to this, what are you saying 'no' to?
- What's possible here, and who cares/doesn't care?
- What is your main inner obstacle?
- We seem to be at an impasse; perhaps should we spend more time exploring more options?
- What if time/power ... wasn't an issue?
- If money was no option, what would you do then?
- What's holding you back?
- If you had a magic wand and could grant yourself any wish, what would it be?
- Whom do you admire or respect who does this really well?

- How would Indra Nooyi/Superman/Mahatma Gandhi/your middle school teacher/Martin Luther King, Jr./Marie Curie/Mother Theresa/Jeff Bezos/your primary competitor ... handle this situation?
- What pointers would you give someone else who's dealing with the same problem?
- If you could do anything you wanted, what would you do?
- What can you do?
- What else could you do?
- What else could you do differently?
- What options can you create?
- What's just one more possibility?
- For instance?
- Like what?
- Such as?
- How does it fit with your goal(s)?
- Any (more) alternatives?
- Which option(s) would add the most value?
- What else can you think of?
- Imagine you're in a helicopter right now hovering *above* this issue ... What can you see *now*?
- What's the worst case scenario?
- What would happen if you did nothing?
- What's the worst thing that could happen? Can you live with that?
- How could you change yourself so that it wouldn't be a problem?
- What would happen if you did X?
- What are the advantages and disadvantages of each?
- If you couldn't fail, what would you do then?
- ***Your favorite question(s):*** ....

COACHING CONVERSATION STAGE: <u>W</u>AY FORWARD

- Which options will you decide on?
- Which options do you most favor?
- Of all the choices we've figured out, which ones do you think you will go for?
- What do you need to do to increase your will to do this?
- How would you round up the effort up to now?
- What's the first step you'll take?
- Where do we go from here?
- What did you learn today?
- What's your conclusion?

- What's the action plan?
- Can you wrap up what you're going to do and by when?
- What will be the first concrete step toward reaching your goal?
- What action will you take? And afterwards? What are your *next* steps?
- Do you have what it takes to make it happen now/soon?
- What are you going to do differently tomorrow?
- Now which piece would you like to tackle first?
- When and where would you like to start?
- When will you do this?
- To clarify, can you tell me more specifically what you're going to do?
- How does this goal fit in with your other personal priorities?
- How would you like me to hold you accountable?
- Who else should know about your plan?
- Who will keep you on track?
- What support do you need?
- How do you know you're successful?
- How will you measure your success?
- What are you willing to take responsibility for?
- Can you let me know/email/call me once you achieve this?
- Can you forgive yourself once a day?
- Can you be more attentive and listen more this week?
- Can you smile 24 times a day this week?
- Can you list 24 things you're happy about every day this week?
- Can you do away with _____ words from your lexicon this week?
- Can you add _____ words to your lexicon this week?
- Can you say "yes"/"no" _____ times every day this week?
- Can you say "thank you" _____ times every day this week?
- What was most useful for you?
- ***Your favorite question(s):*** ....

Disciplined learning launches

Testing is a necessity – whether in school, in marketing, engineering, or science. It's like dipping a toe into the bathwater – better to find out early if it's too cold or hot. What is important in testing is that it gives feedback and encouragement. This feedback must be viable ... and the following is a good tool to ensure the obtained information is valid.

Before rollout, run a series of disciplined learning launches to de-risk change initiative execution – spend a little and learn a lot. Iterate, capture insights, reassess launch, and update/fine-tune/reframe concept(s). Do it in stages (Tables R5.1, R5.2, R5.3, and R5.4).

Table R5.1 Disciplined learning launch design, first stage

Disciplined learning launch design		
Bold hypothesis to test	*Experiment strategy*	*Learning launch # 1*
The concept: Is it ... VRINSE?	Thought Test: Analyzing existing data (Time span: 1–2 days)	Who:
		What:
Valuable		
Rare		How:
Inimitable		
Non-substitutable		When:
Scalable		Where:
Executable		
Have predictions improved/failed?: Invalidating data/Unknowns:		How much:

Table R5.2 Disciplined learning launch design, second stage

Bold hypothesis to test	*Experiment strategy*	*Learning launch # 2*
The concept: Is it ... VRINSE?	2D/3D: 90-minute Co-Creation/ Rapid Prototyping Sessions with some 10–20 target users (Time span: 2–5 weeks)	Who:
		What:
Valuable		
Rare		How:
Inimitable		When:
Non-substitutable		
Scalable		Where:
Executable		
Have predictions improved/failed?: Invalidating data/Unknowns:		How much:

Table R5.3 Disciplined learning launch design, third stage

Disciplined learning launch design

Bold hypothesis to test	Experiment strategy	Learning launch # 3
The concept: Is it … VRINSE?	4D Alpha Test: Testing a solution, based on a working prototype, with ca. 20–50 live users (Time span: 5–10 weeks)	Who: What:
Valuable		
Rare		How:
Inimitable		When:
Non-substitutable		Where:
Scalable		
Executable		How much:
Have predictions improved/failed?: Invalidating data/Unknowns:		

Table R5.4 Disciplined learning launch design, fourth stage

Bold hypothesis to test	Experiment strategy	Learning launch # 4
The concept: Is it … VRINSE?	Beta Test: Testing a solution, based on a working scalable version, with ca. 50–500 live users (Time span: 10–20 weeks)	Who: What:
Valuable		
Rare		How:
Inimitable		When:
Non-substitutable		Where:
Scalable		
Executable		How much:
Have predictions improved/failed?: Invalidating data/Unknowns:		

6   The Gel WorkBox

10 tools

The Gel WorkBox contents

Gel				
ToolBox	*Dynamic actions*	*Tools, worksheets and exercises*		
GEL WorkBox	**G1.** Continuously model, monitor, and measure progress and performance, basing decisions upon metrics chosen in an open book way	Progress, Performance and Impact Traffic Light System		
	G2. Reward and celebrate quick wins	Gamifying Quick Wins	Crafting Success Challenge	Philharmonic Symphony Orchestra: Marching to Victory
	G3. Integrate change lessons learned	Know-How Assets Transfer		
	G4. Reinforce and sustain the organization's new state	Built to Change	Total Reward Mix: Developing Reward Strategies	Job Re-Imagined
	G5. Keep strategizing to win, and keep self-regenerating through continuous, experiential, social and reflective learning, self-organizing, designing, experimenting, and innovating (including practicing *open* innovation via crowdsourcing, innovation intermediaries, or open innovation software)	Leader's Developmental Portfolio: Continuing Executive Development	Trend-Spotter	

Progress, performance, and impact traffic light system

The traffic light system is a good visualization of how to gauge change progress. The approach is shown below.

Monitor and rate your change initiative progress using a traffic light system of Red, Amber, Green and Blue in Table G1.1. Mark in the color: Red ("off track"); Amber ("issues); Green (in progress); and Blue (success).

Now specify the next steps for each Red ("off track") area in Table G1.2. You may want to think about the Amber areas too.

Using Table G1.3, use the assessment tools to manage in an evidence-based way.

Now evaluate the intervention(s) in Table G1.4.

Apply initiative success metrics in Table G1.5.

Table G1.1 Progress, performance, and impact traffic light system

Progress area/ tasks (think scope/spec, cost, schedule)	Chaotic performance or a shift in the wrong direction/major concerns likely to prevent completion of project	Performance static or unchanging toward the desired direction/minor-moderate concerns about progress in this area	Performance moving in the desired state/ no concerns about progress in this the area	Milestones completed
1				
2				
3				
4				
5				
6				
7				

Table G1.2 Next steps for each Red

Steps	% complete	Start	Finish	Notes

Table G1.3 Assessment tools

Type	Specific case	Impact
Key performance indicators (KPIs)		
Focus group		
Employee interview		
Attitude poll		
....		
....		
.....		

Table G1.4 Evaluation

Level	To evaluate	To research	Expected outcomes/evidence
1	Reaction and satisfaction	Did they/we like it? Are they/we happy?	
2	Learning	Did they/we learn much?	
3	Behavior and on-the-job application	Can they/we apply new knowledge/skills/insights in the workplace?	
4	Business impact and (in)tangible results	What's the: • Return on Investment (ROI)? • Return on Expectations (ROE)? • Other intangible benefit?	

Table G1.5 Initiative success metrics

Measures	Quantitative	Qualitative	Leading	Lagging	Input	Output	Financial	Non-cost

Gamifying quick wins

This is a further approach to dealing with change. In convoluted dealings, it is often easy to lose sight of the purpose and the activity that is ongoing. "Gamifying" (as shown below) helps to overcome this dilemma.

5Ws+1H: Who-what-where-when-why-how field game/app

Design and develop a "5W+1H" game/mobile "check-in" app that would capitalize on learning and drive better know-how assets transfer within the enterprise, handle the problem of know-how silos, as well as reward employees for excellent performance in the field. Know-how assets are the accumulated intellectual resources that an enterprise has, including information, ideas, learning, understanding, organizational memory, insights, cognitive and technical skills, and capabilities.

To earn rewards, employees 'check-in' and share WHO exactly they were meeting with on the road, WHAT exactly they talked about, WHERE exactly it occurred, WHEN exactly it took place, WHY exactly it happened, and HOW exactly it went. Complete Table G2.1.

The mobile app transfers employees' data, as well as achievements onto the enterprise internal/social network. The tool allows them to showcase their fieldwork to peers and senior colleagues. Progressively, a healthy competition is encouraged, with employees competing to earn extra points and badges that will boost their status and credentials and increase their ranks on the corporate leaderboard.

Quick wins project list

Now complete Table G2.2, the quick wins project list.

Table G2.1 Five Ws and 1 H

5 Ws and 1 H	Important information/circumstances
Who is it about/with?	
What happened?	
Where did it take place?	
When did it take place?	
Why did it happen?	
How did it happen?	

Table G2.2 Quick wins project list

Quick win achieved by	New know-how asset that can improve enterprise	Priority area for resource allocation (H/M/L)	Rank/reward (points, badges, leaderboards)	Celebration

Crafting success challenge

A challenge is a situation that tests someone's capabilities, a team challenge is more. It helps in developing brainstorming skills, but also aids in building positive team-working skills and creating unit cohesion. Below are proffered some success challenges.

1. To celebrate your initiative success/(quick) win, go away on a corporate retreat. Apart from your usual corporate party, as a team of 4–7 members, design, for example, a new screensaver for the organization's computers (Figure G2.1). It must reflect the theme of your initiative success/(quick) win and be in harmony with the company's purpose. At the end of the design phase, present your design projects to the rest of the group explaining what you have created and what it stands for. Vote to select the best design project, and award a prize to the winning design team. If you wish, use the screen savers in the workplace.
2. Alternatively, distribute plain white T-shirts and a set of laundry marking pens. As a team of 4–7 members, design, for example, a corporate

Figure G2.1 Screensaver template

Figure G2.2 Crest template

crest and draw it on all your T-shirts (Figure G2.2). It must reflect the theme of your initiative success/(quick) win and be in harmony with the company's purpose. At the end of the design phase, model your T-shirts to the rest of the group explaining what you have designed and what it stands for. Vote to select the best design project, and award a prize to the winning design team. If you wish, make the winning team T-shirts for all employees, and proudly wear them at work.

Philharmonic symphony orchestra: marching to victory

Here, more suggestions are offered on building team cohesion, but the twist is that what's on offer are ways of boosting creativity – and ways to enable the spotting of the creative – a set of individuals very necessary to have at hand.

To celebrate your initiative success/(quick) win(s), rent a theatre and invite your employees. Stand up and make room around yourselves (put your arms straight out in front of you, as far as you can reach – this is your peripersonal

Figure G2.3 Purple star

space). Imagine that you are the "Leader of the Band," and are conducting the celebrated New York Philharmonic Symphony Orchestra for the next 4 minutes. Listen to a march by John Philip Sousa, who was known as the March King, and energetically lead the orchestra in unison (recommended march selection: "Semper Fidelis," "The Washington Post," "The Thunderer"). Award the best performer a purple star (Figure G2.3).

Alternatively, at the start of performance, form a Philharmonic Symphony Orchestra Awards Committee to nominate, and vote for, employees who have excelled in leading the enterprise orchestra. Award winner(s) with a certificate (Figure G2.4).

Know-how assets transfer

For continuous improvement, growth, and innovation

The strength of any enterprise lies in its people – and its people working as a well-functioning team. This means that information must be freely exchanged, and through consensus what works brought to light and put into practice. Know-how assets transfer is the way to do this.

1. To transfer *know-how assets*, integrate lessons learned and create new knowledge, follow a "5 E" process (Figure G3.1), which shows the

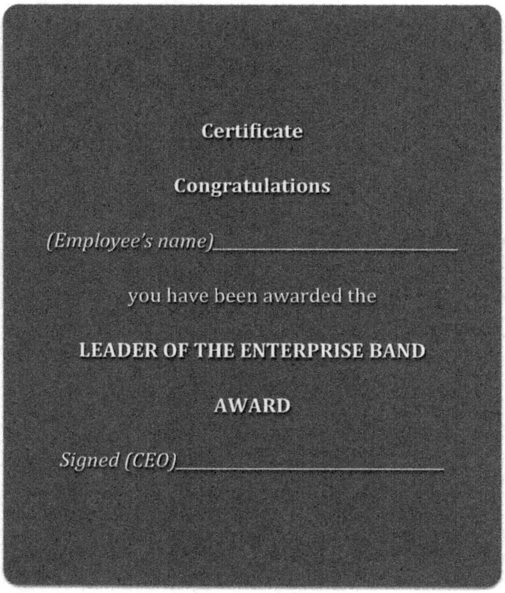

Certificate

Congratulations

*(Employee's name)*_____

you have been awarded the

LEADER OF THE ENTERPRISE BAND

AWARD

*Signed (CEO)*_____

Figure G2.4 Certificate

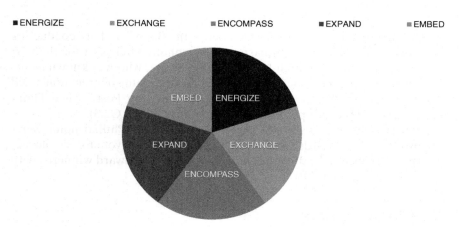

■ENERGIZE   ■EXCHANGE   ■ENCOMPASS   ■EXPAND   ■EMBED

Figure G3.1 "5 E" know-how assets

five modes of Energize/Exchange/Encompass/Expand/Embed (Table G3.1).

2. Add in more examples of identifying, capturing, organizing, and utilizing know-how assets so that they are not lost if they are not well-logged, or when employees are relocated, or when some just leave the enterprise.

Table G3.1 "5 E" know-how assets transfer

"5 E" Know-how assets transfer

Energize	Exchange	Encompass	Expand	Embed
• Mobilize know-how through direct experience, social networking, informal meetings, (reverse-) mentoring, role-modeling, thought-showering, performing market analyses and change conversations	• Exchange know-how through further dialogic reflection, after-action and project reviews, open source software, databases, wikis, podcasts and videos, organization development activities, building frameworks, master classes, best practices, co-creation sessions	• Encompass know-how through e-libraries, conferences, and thought-leadership publications	• Developing new know-how through research, open innovation, crowdsourcing, process simplification, re-design, simulation, feedback and experiments that lead to *next* practices	• Learn and embed know-how in practice through action, contextualizing newly- agreed routines, team coaching, instant feedback, storytelling, and facilitation of learning and development activities • Link change to strategy, organizational performance and leadership
....	....			....
....	....			.....

Built to change

Change cannot survive by itself. It must be reinforced and sustained in order to actually be well-managed, and the old ways banished to corporate history. Table G4.1 tells you how to do this. Reinforce and sustain the organization's new state. To crystalize, it must become the new normality. Reflect on your experience of change and rate each action item with regard to how positively you reinforce and sustain the new normality.

Table G4.1 Built to change

Action	Quality of reinforcing and sustaining the organization's new state				
	Very positive	Positive	Neutral	Negative	Very negative
Winning hearts and minds					
Procedure adopted to deal with (very) negative:					

(Continued)

Action	*Quality of reinforcing and sustaining the organization's new state*				
	Very positive	*Positive*	*Neutral*	*Negative*	*Very negative*
Modeling the way – people are watching you					
Procedure adopted to deal with (very) negative:					
Monitoring and measuring progress					
Procedure adopted to deal with (very) negative:					
Optimizing/Re-modeling					
Procedure adopted to deal with (very) negative:					
Navigating power, politics, and resistance					
Procedure adopted to deal with (very) negative:					
Rewarding wins					
Procedure adopted to deal with (very) negative:					
Celebrating and making it fun					
Procedure adopted to deal with (very) negative:					

Action	Quality of reinforcing and sustaining the organization's new state				
	Very positive	*Positive*	*Neutral*	*Negative*	*Very negative*
Integrating the lessons learned and feedback					
Procedure adopted to deal with (very) negative:					
Learning, relearning and unlearning – also from failures					
Procedure adopted to deal with (very) negative:					
Continuously strategizing, improving, experimenting, and innovating (including practicing open innovation via crowdsourcing and open innovation software)					
Procedure adopted to deal with (very) negative:					

Total reward mix (TRM)

Developing reward strategies

A reward is a benefit for having achieved something positive. Reward strategies help to attract staff, to retain staff, to recognize staff, and to drive positive strategic change. In Table G4.2, you'll find out more about this.

Use rewards to reinforce and sustain the organization's new state, as well as to incentivize and motivate behavior. The reward system should be assessed and (oftentimes) redesigned, as almost every organizational change initiative necessitates some adjustments therein. Remember, the reward system is to showcase value – and the reward should go to the actual individual or team members who generated the positive – not the one who ... umm ... "looked" like they did the job!

Table G4.2 Total reward mix: developing reward strategies

Pay Element (PE-9)	"Before change" state	"After change" adjustments
1. Basic rate (irreducible minimum rate of pay)		
2. Plussage (e.g. payments for educational qualifications, for supervisory responsibilities)		
3. Benefits (e.g. company cars, cafeteria plans, company childcare, private health insurance, occupational pensions)		
4. Premia (e.g. for working at inconvenient times)		
5. Overtime (e.g. fixed or 10–50% more than the normal rate)		
6. Incentives (e.g. payment-by-results schemes, performance-related payment)		
7. Bonus (e.g. holiday bonus)		
8. Setting pay (e.g. job evaluation, external market comparisons, internal labor market mechanisms, collective bargaining)		
9. Salary progression (e.g. manual, skilled manual, admin, tech, pro, management, execs; entry, developing, working, senior-team leader, specialist-manager, principal-director)		

Total reward package

To make work more "rewarding," in regard to reward policies and practices, go beyond pay. Institute and map rewards onto the six sectors: individual, transactional, relational, communal, expected, and unexpected, taking equal account of *tangible* and *intangible*, as well as *extrinsic* and *intrinsic* rewards (Table G4.3).

Table G4.3 Total reward package

INDIVIDUAL	TRANSACTIONAL
Praise	Flexibility
Base pay	Pensions
Contingent pay (Task,	Healthcare
Commitment, Completion,	Holidays
Performance-contingent)	Other perks
Incentives (Cash, Shares, Stock	...
options)	
Bonuses	
Responsibility	
Autonomy	
Promotions	
...	

RELATIONAL	COMMUNAL
Relatedness	Gamified systems (e.g. Points, Badges,
Constant learning and development	Leaderboards)
(L&D)	Recognition and achievement
Feedback loops and reinforcement	Corporate citizenship
(Reverse) mentoring	Corporate values
Career development	Employee voice
Training	Job design
...	Choices
	Leadership
	Work-life integration (WLI)
	...

EXPECTED (Most of the rewards)	UNEXPECTED ("Surprise" rewards)
...	...

Rank and apply rewards in order of "impact on staff" (minimum to maximum)/"advantage for organization" (most to least).
MAXIMUM IMPACT ON STAFF/MOST ADVANTAGEOUS TO ORGANIZATION (e.g. cheapest)

Prestige (e.g. status, coolness, image value)
Give more examples

....

Unique access (e.g. having access to an extra social network)
Give more examples

....

Authorization (e.g. being enabled to create or do certain things others cannot do)
Give more examples

....

Tangibles (tangible rewards)
Give more examples

....

MINIMUM IMPACT ON STAFF/LEAST ADVANTAGEOUS TO ORG (e.g. most costly)

Job re-imagined

A job is a combination of tasks and the relationships that come with performing these tasks. Now, let's look at where you stand in the system and your job – and what positive change has to offer. In Table G4.4, you'll find a well-thought-out way of actively re-imagining your own job to better suit your values, strengths, and passions, leading to greater enjoyment, meaning, and higher performance.

Analyze the current state of your job. Is it excellent (5), above average (4), average (3), below average (2), poor (1), or extremely poor (0)? How much Time (T), Care (C), and Energy (E) do you spend on the tasks involved in your job? Illustrate the current state through brief examples.

Job Conditioning Promise Score (JCPS)

Now calculate your Job Conditioning Promise Score (JCPS).

$(JTI + JTS + SV): 3 = \underline{\hphantom{xxxx}} \times A \times R = \underline{\hphantom{xxxx}}$

Job desired state

Now picture your job being much more energizing, efficient, meaningful, motivating, and satisfying (Table G4.5). Re-imagine your job by making positive changes to its design. How much Time (T), Care (C), and Energy (E)

Table G4.4 Current job state

Current state		
Core job characteristics	*Perceived job conditioning (Reflect and assess the extent to which each job characteristic represents the current state of your job, rating from 0 (extremely poor) to 5 (excellent). Give examples to support your position)*	*Amount of T, C, E Allocated: XL (extra large), L (large), M (medium), S (small), XS (extra small)*
Job Task Identity (JTI) – the degree to which a task requires completing a whole piece of work		
Job Task Significance (JTS) – the degree to which the job has an impact on others (organization, employees, customers)		
Skill Variety (SV) – the extent to which the tasks require a range of skills.		
Autonomy (A) – the extent to which the individual has discretion to make decisions about how it is done		
Relationships (R) – connecting and feedback		

Table G4.5 Job re-imagined

Desired state		
Re-imagining	*Consider renewal enablers (talents, passions, motivators)*	*Amount of T, C, E allocated: XL (extra-large), L (large), M (medium), S (small), XS (extra small)*
Job Task Identity (JTI)		
Job Task Significance (JTS)		
Skill Variety (SV)		
Autonomy (A)		
Relationships (R)		

would you like to actually allocate to your tasks to go with your talents, passions, and motivators?

Action redesign and roadmap

After a month/quarter, calculate your JCPS anew. Compare your "after redesign" score with your "before redesign" one.

$$(JTI + JTS + SV) : 3 = \underline{\hspace{2cm}} \times A \times R = \underline{\hspace{2cm}}$$

- Did JTI, JTS and SV result in experienced meaningfulness of the work?
- Did A lead to experienced empowerment/responsibility for the outcomes of the work?
- Did R generate more feedback from job?

Make some roadmap notes, i.e., action steps over the next week/month, enablers, constraints, success metrics to motivate for change.

Leader's developmental portfolio: continuing executive development (CED)

Positive organizational and personal change can start with self-generated insight – self-change, and can come from within. Being honest with oneself allows for development – first,we have to see the need for change and how to shape it ... "Checking in" with yourself regularly and planning help to cultivate positive change leadership, to self-coach and learn by self-insight, to micro-transform and self-change.

Here is an example: Kevin Krafti, VP of Operations, AWESOME, LLC (a fictional PR boutique) is going to check in on himself in the leader's developmental portfolio (Table G5.1). Create your own "check-in" too.

CED design

Next, craft your future-oriented learning and development in Table G5.2, using the example given.

Trend-spotter

There are ways and means of spotting what's going on in this world so as to be in the best spot to take advantage of it – being on the crest of the wave. But the signs of the change to come are often elusive and misleading. The tool in Table G5.3 helps clear away the fog. You should be STEEPLED (Social, Technological, Economy, Environment, geoPolitics, Law, Ethics, Demographics), to research and monitor the local/national and global environment.

Table G5.1 Leader's developmental portfolio: continuing executive development (reflective "check-in")

Name:.................... Period from:.............. To:..................

Key dates of critical incidents	What happened?	For what reason?	How did/do I feel about it?	What did I figure out?	How have I applied/ will I apply this?	What could I do differently in the future?	Other notes
On Monday, 09.00am. ...	I shouted at one of my direct reports in front of a manager.	I got crazed and distracted. It was stupid, really. ...	I felt really sorry afterwards. I still do actually. I should never have done that!	I feel overwhelmed - too often! I should have slowed down and thought. I truly need to work harder on my positive leadership presence, and building and sustaining high-quality connections at work.	I apologized to him sincerely, asked forgiveness, and promised to act ethically and professionally. I saw my doctor for Attention Deficit Trait (ADT) checkup. I read an article on Emotional Intelligence, and decided to attend a Building Workplace Relationships Certificate Program.	To keep calm, meditate in the morning before work. Go jogging at least three mornings a week. Pay attention to the moments when I feel stressed out and overloaded. Make gratitude notes a daily practice. Implement an ongoing Personal Management Interview (PMI) program, and hold monthly one-on-one meetings with my direct reports.	Hmm, perhaps I need a coach??? ...
At the beginning of May.	I took a 10-day crash course in Arabic, and I made it!	My partner and I will be taking a vacation in Dubai.	Energized and proud. ...	Actually, I got a kick out of doing it. Plus, I discovered I learned enough to be able to book a hotel, order food and drinks, shop for clothes and presents, ask and understand directions in Arabic.	Aside from having fun on vacation, I now want to become a fluent Arabic speaker. My company has just won a very important client in the UAE and Arabic will be critical soon.	Enroll for a certificate language course.	I think I'll add learning Arabic to my Continuing Executive Development (CED) Design!

Table G5.2 Your developmental portfolio: continuing executive development (future-oriented "design")

Name:.................... Period from:................ To: ....

What do I aim to still learn and develop?	What exactly will I do to execute it?	What resources will I require?	Can I identify key enablers? Who is likely to back me up?	What major barriers may I come up against? How may I deal with them strategically?	How will I measure my success?	Who will hold me accountable?	What will my target dates for initiative completion, extension, recycle, or termination be?	Evaluation	Other notes/ Reminders/Red flags
I want to learn how to be more creative, and think like a designer in particular.	I'll join the Design Management Institute, and will order *Design Management Journal*. I'll take a Design Thinking course at a business school. I'll start going to modern art galleries.	Professional membership fee + journal fee. Fee for a 2-day exec ed program (+flights+hotel). One evening per week (free entry).	My company (Actually, I can then discuss most interesting design research and articles with my team members). My partner (In fact, she's into modern art so we could go together.)	Lack of time. Manage energy and time better, plan and make more relevant choices by analyzing my use of time, examining time challenges, identifying ways to leverage my time and managing overload. ...	Organizing weekly 'design jams' at work so that we can chat about design thinking. Certificate of completion. Learning more about modern art techniques so that I'm able to discuss them with experts, too.	My coach. My partner. ...	I'll join the Institute today, and take out an annual subscription to the journal. I'll take my Design Thinking program in October this year. I'll visit a local art gallery this Friday. ...	I'll be asking myself the following questions: Are my organization and I happy? Am I learning lots? Can I now design new products, processes and strategies in a finer way? Do they improve the ratio of usefulness to cost? Does what I do create more customer value?	In the end, I may be thinking of re-crafting our operations strategy (quality, flexibility, delivery, cost objectives, mission, distinctive competence, process policies) so that it's better guided by both our corporate and business strategy.

Table G5.3 STEEPLED

Trend area (STEEPLED)	Possible sources of information (local/national)	Possible sources of information (global)
Social		
Technological and Industrial		
Economy (macro and micro)		
Environment and climate fluctuations		
GeoPolitics		
Law and government		
Ethics and corporate citizenship		
Demographics/human migration/income		

Cool-hunting: Anticipate and spot what's cool today and tomorrow (Table G5.4). Give research-based evidence. *Table G5.4* Trend area

Trend area (STEEPLED)	Local/national	Local/national
	Now	Future
Social		
Technological and industrial		
Economy		
Environment		
GeoPolitics		

Law and government

Ethics

Demographics

Trend area (STEEPLED)	Global Now	Global Future
Social		
Technological and industrial		
Economy		
Environment		
GeoPolitics		
Law and government		
Ethics		
Demographics		

"STEEPLED" analysis mapping: Map future opportunities

Map local/national/global opportunities onto the "Un/Likely to Happen" – "High/Low Impact" framework in Figure G5.1.

Practice unpacking trends

The most powerful trends will be in the "High Impact"/"Likely to Happen" quadrant (Table G5.5).

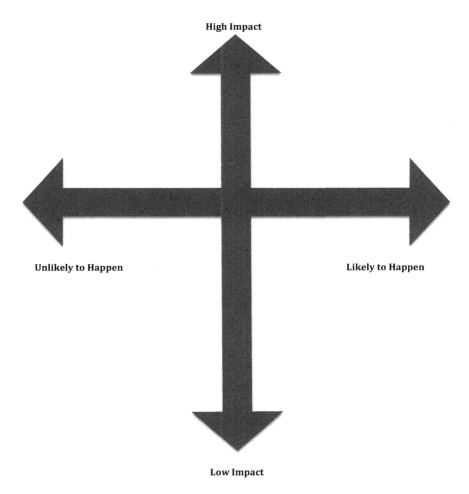

Figure G5.1 Potential future events

Self-regenerate

To self-regenerate, imagine, experiment and design an exciting trend of tomorrow – today. Consider future drivers of change, consumer needs and feelings, expectations, data if already available, as well as "extreme" users. Complete Table G5.6.

Table G5.5 Practice unpacking trends to understand and uncover new opportunities

The Big Ideal/Moonshot

Categories	*Elements*	*Innovation promise*
Drivers of change		
Consumer needs and feelings		
Consumer expectations		
"Extreme" users		
Potential for disruption to shape breakthrough value		
…		

Table G5.6 Self-regenerate

Your *next* big idea that's human-centered (with business rationale and delivery)

Categories	*Elements*	*Degree of riskiness/ complexity*	*Innovation promise*

An open invitation
Let's engage

Way to go! You now have a very good understanding of the practice of leading *positive* organizational change.

In this book, I have offered the framework, processes, tools, and skills necessary for you to effectively craft and execute an organizational renewal strategy that creates a successful new future.

If you like this straightforward, effective, action-oriented, designerly, collaborative approach to empowering *positive*, sustainable transformation and re-imagining your business, why not spread the word to the world? For example:

- You can post something on LinkedIn, Twitter, Instagram, or Facebook.
- You can tell your friends, your colleagues, and your CEO at work.
- You can write a review on Amazon.

Thank you kindly for helping me help more enterprises to lead *positive* organizational change, renew themselves, and achieve superior long-term performance.

If you'd like much more personalized help, let's engage. There are different ways that I engage with individuals, teams, and organizations: as a strategic transformation advisor, a keynote speaker, an executive coach and executive leadership team coach, and an executive educator.

To continue our energizing change conversation, please follow me on Twitter **@DrBTkaczykMBA** and go to **EnergizeRedesignGel.com**. There you can ask questions, read additional positive change stories and case studies, and share your own ideas on positive strategic transformation.

Gratefully,
Bart Tkaczyk

About the author

Bart Tkaczyk is a Fulbright Scholar at the University of California at Berkeley, an Executive Member of the Academy of Management, an award-winning management consultant (trained at Birkbeck, University of London in the UK), a professional executive coach (trained at the Berkeley-Haas School of Business in the USA), and a certified case method instructor and case writer (trained at the Ivey Business School-Western University in Canada).

Working across industries worldwide, Dr. Tkaczyk's strategic management consulting, executive coaching, and public speaking engagements have included projects with AstraZeneca, Bahrain Society for Training & Development, Byblos Bank Group, the Central Bank of Oman, Chipita S.A., Cisco Systems, Dubai Police, the Estée Lauder Companies, Fluor, the Fulbright Program, HP, International Federation of Training and Development Organisations, Lotos, Moody's Analytics, Oracle, Qatar National Bank, Saudi Aramco, Takeda Pharmaceutical Company, UNESCO, the United Nations, among others.

Dr. Tkaczyk has published his research and thought leadership in leading business and strategic management journals in Canada, the UAE, the UK, and the USA, including *Arab Investor, Design Management Review, Development and Learning in Organizations, European Business Review, European Financial Review, Global Business and Organizational Excellence, Ivey Business Journal, Leadership Excellence, Rutgers Business Review, Strategic Change, Strategic HR Review, Talent Development*, and *The World Financial Review*, among others.

Dr. Tkaczyk's professional associations and service, on both sides of the Atlantic, include: the Academy of Management (AOM) in the USA; the Association for Talent Development (ATD) in the USA; the British Academy of Management (BAM); and the Chartered Institute of Personnel and Development (CIPD) in the UK.

Visit drtkaczyk.com
Email bart_tkaczyk@berkeley.edu
Follow twitter.com/DrBTkaczykMBA

Index

Note: **Bold** page numbers refer to tables. *Italic* page numbers refer to figures.

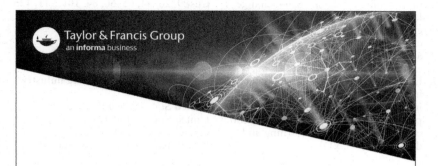

Printed in the United States
By Bookmasters